American

Indian

Women

American Indian Women

PATRICK DEVAL

Translated from the French by
Jane-Marie Todd

Abbeville Press Publishers
New York   London

Front cover: Young Wishram woman. Photograph by Edward S. Curtis, 1910.
Back cover: Zuni girl, from a people of highly skilled potters. Photograph by
Edward S. Curtis, c. 1903.
Front endpapers: Ceremonial and competitive stick game songs, played by
women on a Montana reservation, c. 1910.
Frontispiece: Painted canvas showing a Cheyenne woman during the sun
ceremony.
Back endpapers: Group of Blackfoot women at the White House.
Photograph by Herbert A. Trench, 1923.

For the original edition
Editor: Audrey Demarre
Design: Eric Blanchard

For the English-language edition
Editor: Shannon Connors
Copy editor: Ashley Benning
Production manager: Louise Kurtz
Cover design and typographic layout: Misha Beletsky

First published in the United States of America in 2015 by
Abbeville Press, 116 West 23rd Street, New York, NY 10011

First published in France in 2014 by Éditions Hoëbeke,
7, rue d'Assas, 75006 Paris

First edition
10 9 8 7 6 5 4 3 2 1

Library of Congress Cataloging-in-Publication Data

Deval, Patrick.
 [Squaws. English]
 American Indian women / by Patrick Deval.—English-language edition.
    pages cm
 Originally published in French under the title: Squaws: la mémoire oubliée.
 Includes bibliographical references and index.
 ISBN 978-0-7892-1247-4
 1. Indian women—United States—History. 2. Indian women—North
America—History. 3. Indians of North America—Social life and customs.
I. Title.
 E98.W8D4813 2015
 305.48'897073—dc23
                    2015020357

For bulk and premium sales and for text adoption procedures, write to
Customer Service Manager, Abbeville Press, 116 West 23rd Street, New York,
NY 10011, or call 1-800-ARTBOOK (U.S. only).

Visit Abbeville Press online at www.abbeville.com.

Contents

Guardians of Tradition

MYTHICAL MATRIARCHY

The enthusiasm of the first European observers for the supposed matriarchy of the Amerindians reveals their inability to comprehend the declared egalitarianism of these peoples. They may have been confused because the practices they encountered contrasted sharply with the condition of European women. It was quite obvious to these learned gentlemen that Indian women enjoyed notable personal freedom, that they had property rights (instead of being property), that they were respected and even represented on governing councils. In view of that extraordinary sense of fairness, Europeans reporting on their social structures came to speak of matriarchy, even gynarchy—hastily, perhaps, since a large variety of social institutions could be found in the vast territory of North America.

The kinship terminology applied in anthropology considers two markers for determining whether a society is matriarchal or patriarchal. The first concerns type of residence. In cases of matrilocal residence, the husband joins his wife's family, which will be able to benefit from his talents as a hunter. Thus assembled around related women, men of different clans cooperate and efficiently provide for the family group. In cases of patrilocal residence, it is the wife who moves in with the husband. Both situations are found across the North American continent, north to south and east to west. Some groups are known to have a matrilocal "honeymoon period" for a few years, before the couple chooses where it prefers to live. A Wyandot woman would pick her partner, who came to live in her clan on a trial basis, showering her with gifts. If the man was deemed suitable, he then joined his partner's family.

Above: Kwakiutl wedding ceremony. Photograph by Edward S. Curtis, 1913.

Opposite: A universal icon: Inuit mother and child in Alaska. Photograph by H. G. Kaiser, 1912.

6

MADONNA of the NORTH
(COPYRIGHT 1918)
H.G. Kaiser
NOME ALASKA

Edward S. Curtis taught the citizens of the United States how to see the
first inhabitants of their country. Inuit family from the Noatak group.
Photograph by Edward S. Curtis, 1929.

The second marker, matrilineal filiation, is not in itself a sufficient cri-
terion for defining matriarchy. Amerindian societies in which affiliation with a
clan is handed down from mother to child are matrilineal without being matriarchal. Within a single tribe, patri- and matrilineal practices can coexist. Among
the Haida of western Canada, for example, the chief's heir was not his son but
rather his sister's son. Mixed kinship systems such as those of the Crow-Omaha—
matrilineal in some cases, patrilineal in others—are the most complex. In them,
no woman can marry into a clan that has already provided a husband to her tribe
within human memory, a way to avoid all consanguinity. Hence, "every time
someone chooses a lineage and obtains a husband from it, all other members are
automatically excluded from the number of husbands available for the lineage in
question, and for several generations," noted Claude Lévi-Strauss (1908–2009),
dizzy in the face of the enormous diversity of kinship structures in the Amerindian world. Endogamy is the real taboo of matrilineal societies. Even now,

Above: Seminole family in a canoe in the Florida bayous, c. 1910.

Left: Fortified Indian village in Virginia. Engraving from Théodore de Bry's *Grands Voyages,* 1585–88.

Opposite: Young bride from the Wishram tribe of Oregon, who made their first contact with Europeans through the Lewis and Clark expedition in 1806. Photograph by Edward S. Curtis, 1910.

Above: An ordinary moment in the life of the Hopi, in front of their pueblo. Photograph by Edward S. Curtis, 1907.

members of the Navajo Nation must not marry or even date members of their own clan, though they may join one of the other fifty Navajo groups scattered across their vast reservation.

Most Amerindian societies used the rite of marriage to establish alliances, but unlike in the old regimes of Europe, spouses had no inherited privileges. The husband of an Iroquois matron had no prerogatives associated with his wife's status, and no title was bestowed on the wife of a Delaware chief. Seventeenth-century chronicles mention that Awashonks, the famous Rhode Island sachem, or chief, who supported Metacomet (King Philip, c. 1639–1676) in his war against the English, was the second of the three wives of a "commoner." In matrilineal cultures, marriage was not necessarily the strongest bond between two people. The loss of a parent could be considered greater than that of a husband or wife. The relationship between brothers and sisters of a single tribe often proved stronger than those between husband and wife. Since clan membership is passed from mother to child, the father and his child do not belong to the same clan, but a child and his or her maternal uncle do. Maternal uncles were considered closer to their nieces and nephews than fathers who belonged to different tribes. It was

Above: Everyday life on the mesa: harvest time in Ohkay Owingeh. Photograph by Edward S. Curtis, 1905.

Opposite: Edward S. Curtis photographed a number of Indian mother and child pairs throughout his life; here, Apsaroka, 1908.

usually the uncle who educated his nephews. These customs tended to reinforce clan bonds and provide a stable world for the children, should the parents separate or should one of them die. The extended and recomposed families of Amerindian societies protected the widow and orphan.

Not all groups followed the matrilineal system. In tribes with patrilineal filiation such as the Omaha, the Osage, and the Ponca, the chiefdom was hereditary, passing through the male line, and the children belonged to the paternal clan. For that reason, when someone of European descent took an indigenous wife from one of these groups, their children were classified as "white" like their father or were considered "mixed blood." They did not find a place among their mother's people unless they were adopted.

According to the theorist of matriarchy Johann Jakob Bachofen (1815–1887), women liberated themselves from the tyranny of male sexual caprices by means

of religion, using the "mystery" of maternity to govern the primitive horde and to favor the survival and continuity of the human race. Motherhood fostered women's imaginations: women became the first artisans, inventing pottery to cook and store food, braiding baskets to transport provisions and mats to serve as makeshift shelters. In that braiding lies the origin of weaving cloth. At first, women's power was nurturing and healing. The world of women and the plant world were inextricably linked. The survival of the tribe depended on women's botanical knowledge. In the many Amerindian stories that tell of a wife amassing food reserves while her husband starves to death, anthropologists have identified a striking cultural invariant that illustrates men's feeling of insecurity when confronted with women's domestic power. Guardians of the clan's food, women actively participated in

Santa Clara Pueblo potter. Photograph by Edward S. Curtis, 1905.

Navajo weaver. Photograph by Edward S. Curtis, 1905.

commerce, managing the distribution of surpluses among the group's members. It was the women who, through their symbiotic attachment to their children, made survival possible during the first months of life, and it was they who instituted and transmitted the first forms of articulate language. Nothing has changed in that respect. Beverly Hungry Wolf (b. 1950), a Blackfoot teacher and writer, notes: "I think history about Indians has often neglected the women. We get the impression that women just did their daily work and drudgery and had nothing to look forward to or talk about. When I was young I used to think that the old-time Indian women were sold and treated like slaves, because that's what the books said. I have found out that among some tribes the women were not too well treated, but among others they were equal to the men and among some they even served as chiefs and leaders."

THE THREE SISTERS: CORN, SQUASH, AND BEAN

A very long time ago three sisters, very different in size and appearance, were growing in a field. The youngest, dressed in soft green, was only crawling. The second wore a brilliant yellow robe and, in a manner all her own, presented herself to the sun in the caressing breeze. The third, the eldest, was draped in a pale green shawl, her long blond hair waving in the wind. She stood high and straight above her two sisters to protect them. These three sisters loved one another and would not be separated. One day, a bold Mohawk boy passing by piqued their curiosity by singing to the birds. At the end of the summer, the youngest sister disappeared, to the great sadness of the other two. A little later, the young Mohawk singer was back in the field to gather reeds at the water's edge. The two remaining sisters spotted his moccasin prints. In the night, the second sister—the one who wore a yellow robe—also disappeared. The eldest sister now stood alone in the field. When the Mohawk boy saw her withering away, he felt sorry for her and hastened to reunite the three sisters as he had found them. That is how the Mohawks understood that these three sisters were inseparable and that their strength lay in unity.

The desert plateau of Cajon Mesa in the Four Corners region of Arizona, Utah, Colorado, and New Mexico is soaked by seasonal torrents rushing through the deep canyons. In about the 1200s, the Ancestral Puebloans, an Amerindian nation that vanished before the arrival of the Spanish, came to settle near springs

Left: Young Mohave girl in a cornfield, about 1900.

Right: Bulrush gleaner. Photograph by Edward S. Curtis, 1908.

Opposite: Indigenous agriculture in the Canyon del Muerto of the Navajo. Photograph by Edward S. Curtis, 1906.

Winnowing of grain at the Ohkay Owingeh Pueblo.
Photograph by Edward S. Curtis, 1905.

along the canyons, where they built the village of Hovenweep. The ruins of a tower and several stone buildings still mark one of the most ancient human settlements on the North American continent. Despite the unforgiving environment, the Ancestral Puebloans cultivated "the three sisters"—corn, squash, and bean—as the basis of their diet. Their gardens, arranged on terraces along the canyon, were protected from the wind, irrigated by the water streaming down the walls, and heated by the rocks, and they produced abundant harvests. The gardeners of Hovenweep dug canals to prevent soil erosion and pools to hold the precious water. Historians estimate that the food production of the Ancestral Puebloans was enough to sustain them and even to provide reserves for bad years.

The Pueblo Indians of the southwestern United States still cultivate gardens. The Hopi and Zuni claim to be descended from the ancient Ancestral Puebloans and to have inherited the horticultural knowledge of their women. Even among their more nomadic Apache neighbors, only maternal ancestry is taken into account in filiation. The Apache comprised some sixty-two clans, whose members claimed mythic female creatures as their ancestors. These clans were named after the horticultural sites that the deities had established: for example, "the people of the two rows of yellow spruce growing together."

Mastering the cultivation of grain, whether wheat in Egypt and Mesopotamia, rice in China and India, or corn in Mesoamerica, has often been seen as a stage necessary for the development of civilization. Where North America is concerned, it is often forgotten that the practice of cultivating corn, having originated in Central America, traveled up the great Mississippi River early on, and that most of the pre-Columbian peoples, from the East Coast to the Great Lakes, adopted it. The Pawnee of Kansas, very competent horticulturists, grew nearly ten varieties of corn, seven kinds of squash, and eight types of beans. The European conquerors' stereotyping of the Indians as backward nomadic hunters obscured civilizations of major importance, the better to justify their obliteration. Anthropologist Alice Beck Kehoe, author of *America before the European Invasions* (2002), challenges both the ideology of Manifest Destiny, which allowed the predation of supposedly virgin territory, and the distortions of North American history as written by the victors. She argues that the Europeans who crossed the continent encountered not only primal forests and wilderness but also landscapes and resources made possible by millennia of human activity. Recent archaeological excavations have revealed periods of continuous progress in the design of stone and bone tools, leatherwork, weaving, farming techniques, and the construction of shelters and uncovered traces of previously unimagined trade networks across the entire continent. Indigenous farmers in Mississippi cultivated the fertile soil of the river valleys with hardwood hoes. They lived on corn, beans, squash, and sunflower seeds. They complemented their meals with nuts, berries, fruit, and game (deer and turkey). They caught fish or turtles and collected shellfish in the

Horticultural work in the Caribbean.
Engraving from Théodore de Bry's
Grands Voyages, 1595.

"How they cook their fish."
Engraving from Théodore de Bry's
Grands Voyages, 1593.

Harvesting wild rice in a canoe for the Kootenai of Idaho.
Photograph by Edward S. Curtis, 1910.

many waterways and lakes of the region. In the sixteenth and seventeenth centuries, European travelers on the Mississippi were astonished to come upon actual cities, those of the Natchez, the last descendants of the Mound Builders, who constructed large artificial burial mounds in the Mississippi River Valley between the ninth and fifteenth centuries. These travelers describe a society that worshipped the sun and practiced human sacrifice and ritual suicide, governed by a chief who oversaw four well-defined social classes. Excavations indicate that in about the year 1000, Cahokia, in southern Illinois—across the river from modern-day Saint Louis, Missouri—had as many as twenty thousand inhabitants. The rich valleys around the cities sheltered large rural populations in permanent villages, with about seventy inhabitants per square mile. This scenario cannot be reconciled with the historical stereotype of a world of savages. Archaeologist Mildred Mott Wedel (1912–1995), a pioneer in ethnohistorical studies of the Great Plains, has established previously unknown connections between the prehistory of North

America and the history of the Amerindian nations up to the conquest. Her work has been used by the Iowa, Wichita, and Missouri peoples to prove their ancestral connections to protohistoric sites and to demand compensation for treaties flouted by the U.S. government. Wedel's innovative archaeological approach has revealed a pre-Columbian agricultural revolution, with the introduction of more productive corn seedlings that matured in 120 frostless days rather than the previous 200; in protected regions, two harvests sometimes allowed similar rates of productivity. The cities on the Mississippi were characterized by flattop rectangular mounds surmounted by temples and charnel houses for the upper classes, and log dwellings forming true towns. These religious and administrative centers made it possible to collect and redistribute food and raw materials. It seems that the sporadic wars the French waged against the Natchez from 1710 until the great Natchez revolt of 1729 contributed to the disappearance of these built-up areas.

Hopi millers preparing cornmeal. Photograph by Edward S. Curtis, 1906.

Oahatika women stopping to rest in the Mojave Desert.
Photograph by Edward S. Curtis, 1907.

"A REPUBLIC IN THE STATE OF NATURE"

Farther to the north, the Iroquois were also ardent horticulturists. Their corn, bean, squash, and sunflower crops constituted more than half their diet. "Squash" and "pumpkin," in fact, are two words from the family of Algonquian languages. The women produced, guarded, and controlled the food. Whereas the men used fire to thin the forests, the fields were women's domain. The vast cornfields surrounding the villages of the Atlantic coast impressed the first European colonists. At the time the first Europeans arrived, all the holidays on the Iroquois calendar celebrated women's activities linked to food: the maple feast, the strawberry feast, the feast of young corn. Hunting was not celebrated.

The Iroquois called themselves "Haudenosaunee" (people of the long-houses). The first colonists measured some of these houses, which could extend some 300 feet in length. The name "Iroquois" was given to them by the French: the word, which means "snakes," was adopted from the Iroquois' Huron enemies. As for the Huron, they were so called because of the boar's head (*hure* in French) suggested by their headdresses. The six-nation Iroquois Confederacy astonished François-René de Chateaubriand and, through him, the world. In his *Voyage en Amérique* (*Journey to America*, 1827) about a trip he took in 1791, he recounts his discovery of a true "republic in the state of nature" among the Iroquois, who had established a constitution, a representative assembly, and a federative pact: "Every family provided a delegate named by the wife, who often chose a woman to represent them: hence the foremost power belonged to the women, and the men were said to be only their lieutenants. . . . The Iroquois believed one ought not to deprive oneself of the assistance of a sex whose astute and clever minds are rich in resources, a sex that knows how to act on the human heart." With this Chateaubriand spread a little more confusion about the "acculturated savage." Although chiefs were traditionally chosen from among the males, women did possess an important decision-making role. The Europeans were surprised to find that the great council of the Huron or Wyandot nation was composed of forty-four women and only four men, who were merely the agents of the women's will.

Iñupiat women cut up a beluga whale in the Kotzebue Gulf of Alaska. Photograph by Edward S. Curtis, 1929.

The U.S. Constitution was influenced by the Constitution of the Iroquois Confederacy, still in force today. Originally, five nations—the Mohawk, Oneida, Onondaga, Cayuga, and Seneca—formed a league, which in colonial times was joined by a sixth, the Tuscarora, a people of the Southeast. The admission of that group suggested to the states of the emerging Union that they should act likewise. At the Albany Congress in 1754, Benjamin Franklin (1706–1790) declared that it was unbelievable that the thirteen colonies could not agree on a political union, when six nations of "ignorant savages" had produced a federative pact. Other principles of the Iroquois Confederacy also inspired the U.S. Constitution, such as the notions of representative government, impeachment, and individual freedom. In 1987 a resolution in the U.S. Senate officially acknowledged the Iroquois influence on American democracy and on the founding fathers of the United States, such as Franklin and Thomas Jefferson (1743–1826), great admirers of their representative democracy and political organization. "The Congress, on the occasion of the two hundredth anniversary of the signing of the United States Constitution, acknowledges the contribution made by the Iroquois Confederacy and other Indian Nations to the formation and development of the United States."

Above: Hopi woman baking piki bread. Photograph by Edward S. Curtis, 1906.

Opposite: A shaman belonging to the Hupa people of northwestern California. Photograph by Edward S. Curtis, 1923.

In addition, it should not be forgotten that, in the late nineteenth century, the women's suffrage movement in the United States was influenced by the discovery of the culture of the suffragists' Amerindian neighbors. Feminist militants such as Susan B. Anthony (1820–1906), founder of the New York newspaper *The Revolution* (1868–72)—whose motto was "The true Republic: men, their rights and nothing more; women, their rights and nothing less"—and Matilda Joslyn Gage (1826–1898), author of *Woman, Church, and State: A Historical Account of the Status of Woman through the Christian Ages; with Reminiscences of Matriarchate* (1893), a radical book that blasted all the figures of God the father, quoted indigenous women in their books and speeches, leading the battle for women's voting rights. Alice Fletcher (1838–1923), after being sent on a mission for the Peabody Museum, recounted the experience she had had in a Sioux tribe under customary law in the 1880s. That suffragist ethnologist proclaimed to the rest of the world that Indian women enjoyed great freedom, that their rights to divorce, to own property, to vote, and to control their reproductive lives were recognized.

LIFE IN THE TEPEES

Let us note once again a singular phenomenon: in the midst of the attempted extermination of the Amerindian race, a few researchers of both sexes set about
meticulously to collect the dying embers of these nations. One of them, the ethnologist Frank Bird Linderman (1869–1938), learned sign language during his
youth among the Crow in Montana, which earned him the name "Sign-talker."
He became a journalist, tried his hand at local politics in an attempt to protect Native Americans, and in 1930 published *American: The Life Story of a Great Indian:
Plenty-Coups, Chief of the Crows*. Linderman also retranscribed *Red Mother* (1932),
the autobiography of Pretty Shield (1856–1944), a Crow medicine woman. In this
unique document on Amerindian life in the nineteenth century, Pretty Shield recalls the happy days of her youth: "A crier would ride through the village telling
the people to be ready to move in the morning. In every lodge the children's eyes
would begin to shine. Men would sit up to listen, women would go to their doors to
hear where the next village would be set up, and then there would be glad talking
until it was time to go to sleep. Long before the sun came the fires would be going
in every lodge, the horses, hundreds of them, would come thundering in, and then
everybody was very busy. Down would come the lodges, packs would be made,
travois loaded. Ho! Away we would go, following the men, to some new camping
ground, with our children playing around us. It was good hard work to get things
packed up, and moving; and it was hard, fast work to get them in shape again,

Tanning hides and smoking meat in a Comanche village.
Painting by George Catlin, 1834–35.

Above: A woman dries fish outside her tepee, about 1910.

Right: Tanning hides, the Ho-Chunk of Wisconsin. Photograph by H. H. Bennett, c. 1900.

after we camped. But in between these times we rested on our traveling horses. Yes, and we women visited while we traveled. There was plenty of room on the plains then, so that many could ride abreast if they wished to. There was always danger of attack by our enemies, so that far ahead, on both sides, and behind us, there were our wolves [scouts] who guarded us against surprise as we traveled."

Tepees or lodges were so well adapted to the lives of nomads who followed the migrations of the bison that they could be dismantled and loaded within fifteen minutes and set up in less than an hour. Zoologist William Hornaday (1854–1937), famous for having saved the American bison from extinction by seeking out the last wild specimens in Montana in 1886, estimated that, with the introduction of horses on the plains, twenty hunters could kill a thousand bison during hunting season, which comes to about fifty apiece. It took three days of work to prepare a hide. Some ten hides were needed for a small tepee, twice that for a large one. A bison produced fifty-five pounds of pemmican, a dried and pounded meat mixed with fat, marrow, and berries that kept well, and which the first travelers to North America found irresistible. Tanning, the softening of leather, and sewing, all arduous

At the Acoma water hole, where the People of the White Rock
have lived continuously since the twelfth century. Photograph
by Edward S. Curtis, 1904.

tasks, were done collectively under the strict supervision of a woman elder, an expert in the matter.

Beverly Hungry Wolf remembers: "There is a special thrill to waking up
in a tipi. I think this has helped make tipi living so popular among many different people in recent years. Even among Indians there is a revival of using tipis
at tribal encampments. Tipis are an aesthetic link to our ancestral past, as well
as being handsome and practical dwellings to camp in. . . . I love to wake up on
an early summer morning to hear some old person singing in one of the lodges.
Another old person will go around the camp circle to announce the day's events,
and to add some words of advice and encouragement. This is our traditional form
of news and information broadcasting." Accounts of Indian camps convey an atmosphere of lightheartedness and freedom. Mary One Spot, a Blackfoot grandmother quoted by Hungry Wolf, recounts: "I got my education from my culture.
My teachers were my grandmothers, and I am really thankful for that. . . . We sure
lived healthy back then. We didn't hardly know about candy or liquor, and those
are two things that spoil the young people today. In those days we didn't have any

The comfort of a bundle of sticks: winter among the Apsaroka.
Photograph by Edward S. Curtis, 1908.

Melted snow quenches the thirst: winter among the Apsaroka.
Photograph by Edward S. Curtis, 1908.

springs or wells. In the summer we got our water from the creeks, and in the winter we just melted the snow or ice. I was raised on snow water, and nowadays you can't even drink it because you'll get poisoned. The air is polluted, even here on the reserve, but back then it was all pure. The cities have grown too big and they spread their poison too far, even out into the wild country. We picked all kinds of wild berries. Serviceberries and chokecherries were our favorites. We would put them out in the sunshine to dry—either plain, or we would pound them with a stone hammer and make them into little cakes. We would gather a lot of wild tomatoes [rose hips] and pound them and then mix them with grease to save for the winter. We did the same with kinni-kinnick berries; we separated the berries from the leaves so we could smoke one and eat the other. "

In those bygone days, women's occupations were seasonal: making sugar and maple syrup in the spring; gathering wild rice and berries in the summer; fishing and hunting small game in the fall; and preparing it for the winter, the season of storytelling.

Harvest time. Photograph by Edward S. Curtis, 1908.

Mohave water-bearer with her child. Photograph by Edward S. Curtis, 1903.

MARRIAGE AND OTHER RELATIONSHIPS

Pretty Shield speaks plainly about her arranged marriage, an ancient custom that is almost universal. She justifies it as a means to avoid incest and to fulfill the requirements of exogamy: "My father had promised me to Goes-ahead, when I was thirteen. When I became sixteen years old my father kept his promise. . . . I had not often spoken to him until he took me. Then I fell in love with him, because he loved me and was always kind. Young women did not fall in love, and get married to please themselves, as they now do. They listened to their fathers, married the men selected for them, and this, I believe, is the best way. There were no deformed children born in those days. . . . And men and women were happier, too, I feel sure. A man could not take a woman from his own clan, no matter how much he might wish to have her. He had to marry a woman belonging to another clan, and then all their children belonged to their mother's clan. This law kept our blood strong."

The great linguist of the Algonquian languages Truman Michelson (1879–1938) studied and published many articles on the language and culture of the Fox tribes, who were deported from the Great Lakes region in 1845. His *Autobiography of a Fox Indian Woman* (1925) presents the intimate viewpoint of a woman from that group on traditional life, rites of passage, and child-rearing. His source, whose name was withheld at her request, recounts how at the age of nineteen her parents imposed on her an old husband she did not like. She divorced him and returned to her former love, who left her a widow at a young age. Over time, she became a

Left: Photograph of a young couple, Situwuka and Katkwachsnea, 1912.

Opposite: At the water's edge. Photograph by Edward S. Curtis, 1908.

respected elder of her Meskwaki tribe, which was deported during this period to a reservation in Iowa.

Although polygyny, which allows a man to have multiple wives provided he can support them, was practiced, polyandry, which permits a woman to have several husbands, was practically unknown to the Amerindians, with the exception of the Inuit of the Far North. The Cherokee called divorce "the separation of blankets," a formality in the Amerindian world, where it was not the custom to return wedding gifts. The Plains Indians divorced as easily as they married, a matrimonial instability that greatly disturbed the first missionaries.

Traditionally, marriage was considered an economic partnership. Mountain Wolf Woman, also called Xéhachiwinga (1884–1960), a young Ho-Chunk from Wisconsin, had to endure a marriage against her will, as she confided just before her death to anthropologist Nancy Oestreich Lurie (b. 1924). Lurie then transcribed Mountain Wolf Woman's life in her own words. *Mountain Wolf Woman, Sister of Crashing Thunder: The Autobiography of a Winnebago Indian* (1961) tells of her childhood at a missionary school, her bad marriage and the nine children she bore, her religious experience with the Peyote Way Church of God, and her fight

Opposite: Two Zuni girls in front of their pueblo. Photograph by Edward S. Curtis, 1903.

Left: Two young Piegan girls sitting in the tall grass. Photograph by Edward S. Curtis, 1910.

Right: The two daughters of Bull Shoe. Photograph by Edward S. Curtis, 1910.

to keep her family afloat when her people were dispossessed of their land and rendered homeless. This twentieth-century account also describes concretely how indigenous institutions functioned, in particular, the determining role played by brothers among the Ho-Chunk and the Sioux in general. Mountain Wolf Woman explains that a girl's suitor literally courted his future brother-in-law in order to be accepted into the family. She also relates how, although she was compelled to obey her brothers for her first marriage, that obedience earned her great freedom for all her later unions.

In *L'origine des manières de table* (*The Origin of Table Manners*, 1968), Claude Lévi-Strauss analyzes the meaning of a mythic theme found among the indigenous peoples of North America, which includes two contrasting series, one depicting brothers in search of wives, the other, sisters in search of husbands. These myths indicate a connection between the enemy's scalp or severed head and the female: "Almost everywhere, scalps were immediately handed over to women or to men whose kinship with the winner was established through the women. Among the forest-dwelling Algonquians as well as the Plains and Pueblo Indians, women performed the scalp dance with blackened faces and often dressed up as warriors. At the end of the dance, they seized hold of the trophies." The interest women displayed in the scalps, which were the affair of men, can be understood as a search for equivalence between the bleeding of the warrior and that of women, a bleeding that both unites and separates them. Sisters who dance in honor of the scalps captured by their brothers exhibit their femininity when their brothers have proven the reality of their masculinity. "If a brave man takes you for his woman," a

Dakota tells his daughter, "you may sing his scalp song and you may dance his scalp dance" (James R. Walker, quoted by Lévi-Strauss).

Among the Cheyenne, scalp dances could be the beginning of love affairs. The ancient custom of elopement was a useful way to get out of arranged marriages. Not all Amerindian girls accepted the suitor chosen by their parents. When a girl allowed herself to be abducted, she could choose her heart's desire despite the arrangements made, and parents could later legitimate the union through an exchanges of gifts. "The crawling lover" is another familiar figure in the stories of certain Amerindian tribes: during the night, he sneaks into the lodge or hut of the woman who appeals to him. That manner of courting, accepted among the Hopi and the Plains Indians, met with intense disapproval from more severe peoples such as the Apache and the Cheyenne, who strictly chaperoned their daughters, and among the Tlingit, who placed a high value on their virginity.

As in many ancient cultures, men often practiced sexual abstinence before leaving for a hunting expedition or for war, to keep up their energy. Sex might also be avoided at certain times of the year: among the Apache, for example, during the season for gathering, preparing, and cooking hearts of the agave, the sacred cactus shared at an annual ritual.

Adolescent Plains Indians were admitted to one of the societies that structured a tribe. Ella Deloria (1889–1971), both an heir to that tradition and an ethnologist, was one of the first women to write between two worlds. She explains how these societies functioned among her people, the Dakota: "The executive Chiefs' Society and the advisory Owl Headdress were composed of elderly, venerable worthies who did much sitting and deliberating. The remaining four, known as Badgers, Stout Hearts, Crow-keepers, and Kit Foxes were military orders ever alert for action. It was not demanded of them, or of any man, to go to war unless he wanted to go. The military orders functioned rather as messengers, scouts, camp police, in short, as guardians of the camp circle and its people. They patrolled and regulated the communal hunt and in every way carried out the orders of the magistrates and council." The Sioux ethnologist goes on to describe the notion of friendship as it existed among her people, with the figure of the *kola,* or "fellow." Two *kolas* formed "a solemn friendship pact that must endure forever," and the needs and wishes of a *kola* could not be ignored. The words, "the best I have is for my fellow," sealed their loyalty. The best horse belonging to one became that of the other. They went on the warpath together and protected each other. A *kola* became the son of his fellow's parents, and other family members were also held in common. Each was therefore the brother-in-law of the other's wife, but with a difference. Whereas actual brothers- and sisters-in-law

Two young Comanche. Painting by George Catlin, 1834.

We-Wa, a Zuni berdache, weaving. Photograph by John K. Hillers, 1907.

could have a pleasant and relaxed relationship, respect and veneration were required for a *kola*'s wife.

Amerindian societies respected transsexuals and transvestites. Their difference was seen as a gift from the gods, and it was their spirit more than their sexual identity that was taken into consideration. Berdaches were honored, entrusted with sacred missions as healers, storytellers, matchmakers, or prophets. Identified in 150 tribes across the entire continent, from the Apache to the Zuni, berdaches, or "two spirits," were more often androgynous men who dressed and behaved like women. Female berdaches existed in a few tribes and participated in the work of the opposite sex—hunting and war—just as male berdaches might engage in weaving and basketwork, women's work. Then came colonization and with it persecution. The Spaniards and later the English considered it an "abominable sin" to be a berdache; the status of a two spirits went from that of a spiritual being to that of a sexual criminal. The field of gender studies has now shed light on the distinction between the biological reality and the social construct. U.S. feminists have argued that one can be a woman biologically speaking and yet invent a gender and sexual orientation for oneself, acknowledging one's desires and the complexity of a world with more flexible boundaries. What we can still learn from the remote customs of the Amerindians is their notion of a society that does not instill fear or threaten individuals who are different but in fact recognizes the contribution they make.

TRADITIONS OF
THE INDIAN ARTS

The bodily freedom of the Native Americans also comes through in their clothing. Although men's trousers and vests were fairly basic, women's leather skirts and dresses contrasted sharply with the cumbersome outfits of colonial women. Let us dismiss from the outset the accepted idea that, in both the animal world and among so-called primitive peoples, the male is more beautiful, showy, and vain than the female, and that only in the modern Western world do women wear more ornaments and makeup. The proud bearing of the great Indian chiefs in their feathered headdresses has obscured the elegance and fine eye for decoration of Amerindian women. Spectators at a modern powwow are privy to a widely shared taste for feathers and makeup. The fringed dresses of the Plains women, like the eagle feather headdresses of their brothers, have come to represent the stereotypical costume for all Indians, for which we have Buffalo Bill and Hollywood to blame. We should instead appreciate the rich imagination and remarkable skill that went into the traditional costumes and jewelry made by indigenous women throughout the Americas. Most pre-Columbian garments, such as skirts, leggings, and moccasins, were made of buckskin, but plant fiber was also much in use. Nettles, hemp, and the inner bark of certain trees were braided and woven to make shirts, bags, and cloaks. The Tsimshian of the Pacific Northwest

Left: Painted canvas showing a Cheyenne woman during the sun ceremony.

Right: Cherokee girl, 1920.

Opposite: Kalispel woman, whose dress is decorated with elk's teeth. Photograph by Edward S. Curtis, 1910.

produced their ceremonial dance blankets, or *chilkat,* from the twisted fibers of
cedar bark. For thousands of years, the autochthonous peoples of North America
domesticated and cultivated a large range of plant species that provided them with
clothing for all seasons.

But it was their passion for ornament that best expressed their artistic sen-
sibility and panache. Ella Deloria tells us that, among the Dakota, all enemies were
received with open arms during the annual feasts and that this courtesy was re-
ciprocated. Dressed in their most beautiful finery, the Amerindians knew how
to incorporate their spirit of celebration into their politics. Glass beads, knick-
knacks, trinkets, trade beads, gewgaws, baubles, trifles: the vocabulary of the first
traders who crossed the oceans eloquently evokes the wealth of decorative ornament found in commerce between Amerindians and colonists. Bead embroidery,
though it dates only to the eighteenth century, is considered a specialty of Amerindian women. Earlier, however, they had used feathers, shells, seeds, claws and
fangs, semiprecious stones, native copper, and porcupine quills, a remarkable collection of natural elements transformed by nimble fingers into sparkling outfits.
Beadwork was soon practiced with speed and skill. The old geometrical motifs
found new life in bead weavings but also in the original use of old silk ribbons

Opposite left: Engaged Sioux woman. Photograph by Edward S. Curtis, 1908.

Opposite right: Umatilla girl from Oregon. Photograph by Edward S. Curtis, 1910.

Right: Betrothed woman in ceremonial dress, Nespelem of the Nez Perce. Photograph by Edward S. Curtis, 1905.

from Europe: by cutting them up and appliquéing them, Native Americans created fantastic new designs that reflected their aesthetic sense. These decorations evolved continually and remain very popular. They can be admired in the ceremonial dress of contemporary powwows.

Wampum, the famous belts woven from porcupine quills and shells, represented the most valuable currency for the Iroquois people. It commemorated events and sealed alliances, and was also worn as jewelry of honor. The Europeans saw wampum as an opportunity to exploit the indigenous peoples' taste for such objects: they manufactured wampum made with colored glass beads, which flooded the market and destabilized the local economy. Quillwork was one of the most refined types of weaving in existence. The weaver dyed porcupine quills, then flattened and cut them, before braiding them through leather strips to create colored motifs. It is said that most Iroquois women used to know that art, but it has now nearly disappeared. The flag of the Iroquois Confederacy still shows a beautiful example of wampum. The Yurok, the Tlingit, and the Haida on the West Coast prized abalone or dentalium, gleaming shells that were long used as currency. Widespread tattoos complemented the outfits of women. Most of the designs and their meanings have been lost.

Young Apache mother and
her baby. Photograph by
Edward S. Curtis, 1903.

Chippewa mother.
Lithograph by Charles B.
King, 1842.

Flattening the skulls of
newborns. Painting by
George Catlin, 1835.

Women held the power of life: they carried their infants on their backs in
cradleboards sometimes engraved with a sun and the North Star and covered with
wildcat skin, a symbol of the starry sky. The board, forming an arc over the child's
head, had a rainbow painted on it. Amerindian cradles came to be included in the
collections of museums; these pieces, more than war gear, allow insights into the
Amerindian peoples.

Moccasins are another of their gifts to the rest of the world. Europeans with
a sharp eye and discerning feet quickly understood the quality of Indian mocca-

Making moccasins, 1900.

sins and adopted the soft-soled shoes for long walks in the forest. In fact, though European shoes of the time were more water-resistant and longer-lasting, they were also more expensive and dried more slowly. In addition, cobblers were still rare in the wide-open spaces of the Americas. For that reason, pioneer children often went barefoot, saving their poor shoes for church and the heart of winter. By contrast, every Amerindian child owned five or six pairs of moccasins, changing them as soon as they got wet. Moccasins were rubbed with fat to waterproof them, and the Iroquois lined them with corn husks. Winter moccasins were sewn with deer hide on the inside and rubbed with bear fat on the outside. It did not require special tools or skills to make moccasins, and it cost very little, a novelty for the Europeans, who could finally change their shoes the way they changed their shirts.

Artisanry was the prerogative of women. Generation after generation, women potters in North America fashioned containers for their people's food, a realm in which they discovered a remarkable creative freedom. With a ball of clay—kneaded, modeled, and decorated—Pueblo Indian women in the Southwest created an original domestic art. María Martínez (1887–1980) was a Pueblo potter who revived that art among her people and fostered an appreciation for it throughout the world. Susan Peterson's *The Living Tradition of María Martínez* (1978) recounts her life. Ruth L. Bunzel's *The Pueblo Potter* (1969) also records the beauty of the art of pottery, continuing to our own time. Among the wonders created by Indian women, their basketwork attests to a refined "first art." Women of the Southwest—Apache, Hopi, Navajo, Paiute, Pima, and Tohono O'odham— braided nets, sacks, mats, and baskets so tight they could hold water. The Pomo of California are known for the decorative genius of their baskets, covered with a mosaic of miniscule iridescent feathers held in place by the weave. How much has been lost with modernization?

A group of Maricopa women from Arizona. Photograph by Edward S. Curtis, 1907.

A Mohave decorates her pot with a yucca brush. Photograph by Edward S. Curtis, 1907.

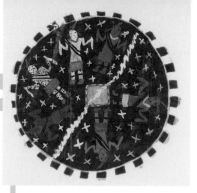

2

Amerindian Spirituality

THE CIRCLE

Remnants of the material culture of the vanished Amerindian peoples decorate our museums to great advantage. Beautiful vestiges of their vision of the world live on in our consciousness. Consider the contemporary awareness of their ecological values, egalitarian societies, and notions of the individual quest. The Amerindian spiritual heritage challenges our way of thinking, especially with respect to the place of women in the sacred circle, both in the heavens and on earth.

Some have expressed astonishment that the first peoples of the Americas did not "invent" the wheel—the loads pulled by their dogs were on travois— even though they venerated the circle and medicine wheels. But wheels require a road that covers the ground, and it was unthinkable to confine one's mother under a paved network, which would also be hard on moccasins and hooves. Nevertheless, ancient transcontinental trade routes did exist in pre-Columbian North America, as attested by precious materials such as obsidian blades from Alaska found in California excavations. It is also known that engineers built the western highways over the tracks inscribed in the landscape by the transhumance of enormous bison herds across great spans of time. The continent, with its generous hydrographic network, was irrigated by multiple communication routes. Even without horses, indigenous peoples did not have to undertake Roman-style works projects to travel far and wide. Their wheel remained purely a symbol of cosmic harmony.

Above: Zuni painting symbolizing that group's vision of the world inscribed in a circle, c. 1900.

During an eclipse, Kwakiutl dance to make a heavenly creature spit out
the moon it has swallowed. Photograph by Edward S. Curtis, c. 1914.

Hunting scene and abstract circular symbols engraved two thousand years ago on Newspaper Rock in Utah, a national monument
since 1961, site of a large collection of Amerindian petroglyphs.

Eagles fly in concentric circles toward the sun. Braves smoked the peace pipe in a ring, just as they had circled the enemy. Women's round dances brightened the nights. For the Amerindians, everything took place under a round sky. In their ceremonies, they participated in the circle of life, the circle in its totality, both visible and invisible. They taught that our actions travel in a circle and always come back to us. The shaman's drum that calls on the divine spirits is round, as is the belly of a woman bearing life. "Our tepees were round like the nests of birds, and these were always set in a circle, the nation's hoop, a nest of many nests, where the Great Spirit meant for us to hatch our children. But the Wasichus [non-Indians] have put us in these square boxes. Our power is gone and we are dying .... We are prisoners of war ... but there is another world." Thus spoke Black Elk (1863–1950), a Sioux holy man, survivor of the Battle of Little Bighorn (1876) and the massacre at Wounded Knee (1890). According to holistic Amerindian thought, human beings constitute only one arc of the circle and find their place in relation to the other living beings that compose it: animals, plants, and the natural elements.

The term "medicine wheel" was first used in reference to the Bighorn Medicine Wheel, a megalithic site in Big Horn County, Wyoming. Its circular stone structure, eighty feet in diameter, traces a large wheel, whose hub is marked in the center by a small pile of rocks, from which radiate twenty-eight paved lines. Archaeologists think that the most ancient medicine wheels are more than 4,500 years old. They were abandoned for centuries, then restored by the new generations of Midwestern nations—Kainai, Gros Ventre, Blackfoot, Cheyenne, Crow, Mandan—and by the eastern Algonquian peoples, who are now reviving the rituals associated with these sacred structures. Wheels of life are often perched at the top of small mountains, places for prayer and harmonization with the spirits, where a person can find his or her place on earth. To live in the world, one must make a home in it. The manifestation of the sacred reveals a fixed point, a center,

The Dutch captain Johannes Staden, tied up in the center of a ring of Amerindian women. Engraving taken from Théodore de Bry's *Grands Voyages*, 1593.

Painting on bison leather depicting the sun dance ritual of the Plains Indians, 1885.

Bighorn Medicine Wheel in Wyoming.

Sisterhood is expressed in round dances: Omaha
girls between Iowa and Nebraska, c. 1910.

Gathering of a society of Arikara shamans around a
sacred cedar. Photograph by Edward S. Curtis, 1908.

Ta-vo-kok-i (circle dance) of the Native Americans of Colorado. Photograph by
John K. Hillers on an expedition for the U.S. Geological Survey, 1873.

an opening upward, in relation to which the spiritual being will orient his or her life. The circle traces an optimistic vision of an existence that is periodically renewed and conveys the interconnection of all things. The word "medicine" has been attached to so many aspects of Amerindian religions that it has lost much of its value. "Medicine" means mystery, explained George Catlin (1796–1872), painter of American Indians, comparing it to the medieval "mysteries."

THE FOUR DIRECTIONS

Walking Man (1961), the spindly bronze statue by Alberto Giacometti, represents the human race between heaven and earth advancing toward the horizon—like the ancestors of the Amerindians, who crossed the ice-free corridor of ancient Beringia, the land bridge connecting Asia and the Americas during the ice age. They bequeathed to their descendants the talent for overland wandering that would take them to Cape Horn. They were omnivores, the women and children gatherers, the men hunters, and as such could delight in any environment while exploring, discovering, adapting, or migrating in all four directions of the sacred circle.

Since time immemorial, the first peoples of the Americas have inscribed their cosmos as a circle divided into four quarters, thereby organizing the manifestations of the world's four cycles: the four seasons, the four times of day (morning, afternoon, evening, night), the four phases of the moon, and the four directions. Fortified by that cosmic order, these peoples serenely climbed the four hills of life, those of childhood, youth, adulthood, and old age. Although rites of passage varied by region, most Amerindian peoples of both sexes celebrated these stages in due course, orienting themselves in relation to the four directions. To the east, in the morning, is the first hill, a free land of trust where the child comes to life. Its color is yellow, its season spring, its spirit peaceful and playful. To the south rises the second hill, dressed in red; it symbolizes summer, the quest, and courage. This is the time when the attributes of a fetish animal enter the minds of young initiates and come to form part of their names. The brooding souls of adolescents allow them access to

Hopi kachina dance mask with circle and the colors of the four directions, painted by Wolf Robe Hunt (Wayne Henry), 1928.

visions that will guide them during their lives. The third hill, to the west, is associated with adulthood and the color black. It embodies autumn, rain, and the spiritual heart. It is the hill of the solitary vigil, the quest for signs of the permanent presence of the Great Spirit. To the north, finally, stands the white hill of maturity, wintry and windswept, the emblem of old age, death, and the spirit, the hill where elders transmit their wisdom to the young. Life develops in that quadrant in terms of the circular conception of time.

The Omaha chanted to welcome their newborns: "Ho! You Sun, Moon, Stars, all you that move in the heavens, I bid you hear me! Into your midst has come a new life. Give your consent, I implore you! Make its path smooth, that it may reach the brow of the first hill! Ho! You Winds, Cloud, Rain, Mist, all you that move in the air, I bid you hear me! Into your midst has come a new life. Give your consent you, I implore you! Make its path smooth, that it may reach the brow of the second hill! Ho! You Hills, Valleys, Rivers, Lakes, Trees, Grasses, all you of the earth, I bid you hear me! Into your midst has come a new life. Give your consent you, I implore you! Make its path smooth, that it may reach the brow of the third hill! Ho! You Birds, great and small, that fly in the air, Ho! You Animals, great and small, that dwell in the forest, Ho! You Insects that creep among the grasses and burrow in the ground—I bid you hear me! Into your midst has come a new life. Give your consent you, I implore you! Make its path smooth, that it may reach the brow of the fourth hill! Ho! All you of the heavens, all you of the air, all you of the earth: I bid you all to hear me! Into your midst has come a new life. Give your consent, all of you, I implore! Make its path smooth—then shall it travel beyond the four hills!"

Roland W. Reed, along with Edward S. Curtis, was one of the few photographers who sought to capture the "vanishing" Amerindian world. The Indian soul immersed in nature for this "prayer to thunder." Photograph by Roland W. Reed, 1912.

"Echoes call," a moment of grandiose communion. Photograph by Roland W. Reed, 1912.

Susan LaFlesche (1865–1915), born on the Omaha reservation in Nebraska, was the first medical doctor of Amerindian origin in the United States. In Jeri Ferris's biography *Native American Doctor* (1991), LaFlesche recounts how she was sent by her father, Joseph LaFlesche, to study at the Women's Medical College of Pennsylvania in Philadelphia, where she earned her medical degree. Dr. LaFlesche returned to practice her art at her home reservation for the rest of her life, to treat her people for tuberculosis and alcoholism.

In 1913 she founded Walthill Hospital, the first on an Indian reservation in the United States; it has now become the Dr. Susan LaFlesche Picotte Memorial Hospital and a museum of Omaha and Ho-Chunk cultures. "In reading these legends," she said, "I hope people will try to imagine themselves in a tent, with the firelight flaming up now and then, throwing weird effects of light and shadow on the eager listening faces, and seeming to sympathize and keep pace with the story, and how we have had only these legends and stories in place of your science and literature."

Susan LaFlesche, first Amerindian woman to become a medical doctor in the United States.

AMERINDIAN DUALISM AND THE MARRIAGE OF OPPOSITES

Comparatism has its vices and virtues, but the cultural disparities within the pre-Columbian Amerindian world keep us from making generalizations on a continental scale. Here and there, we can identify adaptive traits shared by peoples of the world who have never been in contact with one another. But whenever the question of "cultural invariants" arises, the revelation of supposed universals of the human psyche can give pause. Even so, structural anthropology provides tools for uncovering constants in Amerindian thought. In Claude Lévi-Strauss's *Histoire de Lynx* (*Story of Lynx*, 1991), his last volume devoted to Amerindian mythology, the author compares tales widespread throughout North America whose principal theme develops the idea of twinship, which can also be found in the most ancient myths of Brazil and Peru. The ethnologist recounts how the distinction between sky and earth, men and women, fog and wind, fire and water, felines and canines, and war and commerce appeared in the earliest times of creation. Here woman is not an afterthought, a supplement made from man's rib. The female world existed from the beginning—the fertile opposite of the male world, different but equal and not subsidiary. On their journey from faraway Asia to the New World, Amerindians carried with them the yin and the yang. Lévi-Strauss believes it is possible to trace the philosophical and ethical sources of Amerindian dualism. "Well before the arrival of the whites, in the dualist thought of the Amerindians, their own existence implied that of the other. The historical evidence confirms this interpretation. From one end of the New World to the other, Indians proved to be extraordinarily well disposed toward welcoming the whites, making

a place for them, providing them with everything they desired and more. That openness to the other explains the hospitality that the Indians initially offered the whites, who, however, were driven by much less friendly motives." The Amerindians, as if expecting the arrival of other beings who would shatter their splendid isolation, were ready to welcome them. Well before they arrived in the New World, the place of the Europeans was marked out in the Amerindian system as a negative space. Several Native American myths tell of a potential rift between twins, who apply themselves to widening

Engraved figurines representing two Haida shamans from the Pacific Northwest. Photograph by Edward S. Curtis, 1915.

Couple in meditation. Photograph by Roland W. Reed, c. 1910.

it, as if a metaphysical need compelled them to distinguish themselves from each other. These myths illustrate the existence of a duality indispensable for the perpetuation of all things: the same always engenders the other; the child is never the clone of its parents. The smooth operation of the universe depends on the disequilibrium within nature and on the differences between beings. A black dot within the white yang and a white dot within the black yin tip the balance and lead to movement.

A myth of the Blackfoot related by anthropologist Paul Radin (1883–1959) illustrates the difference between men and women with a humor that is all too rare: "There was once a time when there were but two persons in the world, Old Man and Old Woman. One time, when they were travelling about, Old Man met Old Woman, who said, 'Now, let us come to an agreement of some kind; let us decide how the people shall live.' 'Well,' said Old Man, 'I am to have the first say in everything.' To this Old Woman agreed, provided she had the second say. Then Old Man began, 'The women are to tan the hides. When they do this, they are to rub brains on them to make them soft; they are to scrape them well with scraping-tools, etc. But all this they are to do very quickly, for it will not be very hard work.' 'No, I will not agree to this,' said Old Woman. 'They must tan the hide in the way you say; but it must be made very hard work, and take a long time, so that the good workers may be found out.' 'Well,' said Old Man, 'let the people have eyes and mouths in their faces; but they shall be straight up and down.' 'No,' said Old Woman, 'we will not have them that way. We will have the eyes and mouth in the face, as you say; but they shall all be set crosswise.' 'Well,' said Old Man, 'the people shall have ten fingers on each hand.' 'Oh, no!' said Old Woman, 'that will be too many. They will be in the way. There shall be four fingers and one thumb on each hand.' 'Well,' said Old Man, 'we shall beget children. The genitals shall be at our navels.' 'No,' said Old Woman, 'that will make child-bearing too easy; the people will not care for their children. The genitals shall be at the pubes.'" The moral of this odd fable of a man who speaks first and thinks later, accompanied by a woman who lets him talk, only to better provide the sensible alternative, is that equality in difference is our lot. Radin, who published *Primitive Man as Philosopher* (1927), was an anthropologist ahead of his time. Along with Carl Gustav Jung (1875–1961), he developed the concept of the "inner child" while studying the psychology of the divine trickster, an atypical civilizing hero who reappears insistently in Amerindian myths. He found that in the cosmological interpretation of the indigenous mind, the realms of the natural and the supernatural, the visible and the invisible, and the animate and the inanimate, communicate and influence one another. Every evening around the fire, the tribe brings its history back to life; its epic becomes flesh.

THE GREAT SPIRIT

"The Black Hills is our church, the place where we worship. The Black Hills is our burial grounds. The Bones of our grandfathers lie buried in those hills," said Frank Fools Crow (1890–1989), ceremonial chief of the Teton Sioux, when invited to offer a prayer before the U.S. Senate in 1975. In his surrealistic invocation to Wakan Tanka in the holy of holies of the conquerors, he said in substance: "In the presence of this house, Grandfather, Wakan Tanka, and from the directions where the sun sets, and from the direction of cleansing power, and from the direction of the rising sun and from the direction of the middle of the day, Grandfather, Wakan Tanka, Grandmother, the Earth who hears everything: Grandmother, because you are woman for this reason you are kind, I come to you this day to tell you to love the red men, and watch over them, and give these young men the understanding because, Grandmother, from you comes the good things; good things that are beyond our eyes to see have been blessed in our midst. For this reason I make my supplication known to you again. Give us a blessing so that our words and actions be one in unity, and that we be able to listen to each other. In so doing, we shall with good heart walk hand in hand to face the future. In the presence of the outside, we are thankful for many blessings. I make my prayer for all people, the children, the women and the men. I pray that no harm will come to them, and that on the great island, there be no war, that there be no ill feelings among us. From this day on may we walk hand in hand. So be it."

Opposite: Canyon de Chelly in Arizona, where the gods of the Navajo reside. Photograph by Roland W. Reed, 1913.

Pre-Columbian North America is sometimes portrayed as a continent untouched by monotheism. Yet the notion of the Great Spirit, of Gitche Manitou, of the Great Master of Life, has emerged from studies of Amerindian religiosity. These so-called pagan nations, without having had a Moses, a Jesus, or a known Messiah, were able to develop reverence, prayers, and the aspiration for transcendence. Amerindian women were on equal footing in speaking of the Great Spirit. Take the example of Ella Deloria, also known as Beautiful Day Woman (1889–1971), who was born on the Standing Rock Indian Reservation of the Yankton Sioux in South Dakota. After being educated by the Episcopal church, she left to study anthropology at Oberlin College in Ohio, then at Columbia University. There she met Margaret Mead (1901–1978) and Ruth Benedict (1887–1948), two students of Franz Boas (1858–1942), the founding father of Amerindian ethnology. Deloria became Boas's assistant and collected a number of legends from the Sioux oral tradition throughout her life. Both heir to the tradition and an ethnologist, Deloria was one of the first Amerindian women to write between two worlds: "But first of all we must know something of the terms they used. The basic Dakota word in this area is *wakan*. God is Wakan. By whatever name a people may call him, he is still the same. I mean that Almighty Power, invisible, but nonetheless real, even to the most primitive. They feel there is a Power greater than themselves, which

Peace, and a reflection mirrored in the water, for this
Navajo woman. Photograph by Edward S. Curtis, 1904.

Ella Deloria was an educator, writer, and the first ethnologist to write between two worlds.

in all ages and climes they strive somehow to understand. The Dakotas called him by various terms: Wakan (Holy, Mysterious, Magical, Inscrutable); Taku-Wakan (Something-Holy); Taku-Škanškan (Something-in-Movement); Wakantanka (Great Holy—commonly translated as the Great Spirit); and, finally, Wahupa, an untranslatable term in the sacred language of the esoteric. . . . Most . . . prayers were more rational, made to a rational medium of Wakan that could be counted on to answer with due respect, honor, and dignity as a man to his relative. The river was always implored as the giver of beauty. The four winds and the earth and the sun were all benevolent mediums." Deloria's name will live on in human memory, thanks to the Deloria crater on the planet Venus applied in her honor, a posthumous beatification granted by science rather than the church.

THE EARTH MOTHER

Anthropological research has discovered that, in the ancient Americas, the condition of indigenous women was more evolved than the persistent early settlement stereotype of the wife as drudge would suggest. Women in those remote times exerted magico-religious powers, thanks to their knowledge of the plant world. It was women who acclimatized and cultivated plants for food. The alchemical powers of nature—whether from plants for nourishment, plants for protection, healing plants, or psychotropic plants—were their prerogative. A feminine gnosis came into being, one that would defy the acculturation desired by the colonists.

If one spiritual entity can be identified among all the first nations of the Americas, it is that of the Earth Mother. Some find it surprising that, in the absence of real agriculture, Amerindians fervently worshipped the Earth Mother, the sacredness of woman as giver of life. In the Americas, human childbirth was merely a variant of telluric creation.

Opposite: "At the fountain":
Ojibwe woman. Photograph by
Roland W. Reed, 1908.

Above: A Cheyenne wise woman
offering the sacred pipe to the earth
during the sun dance. Photograph by
Edward S. Curtis, 1910.

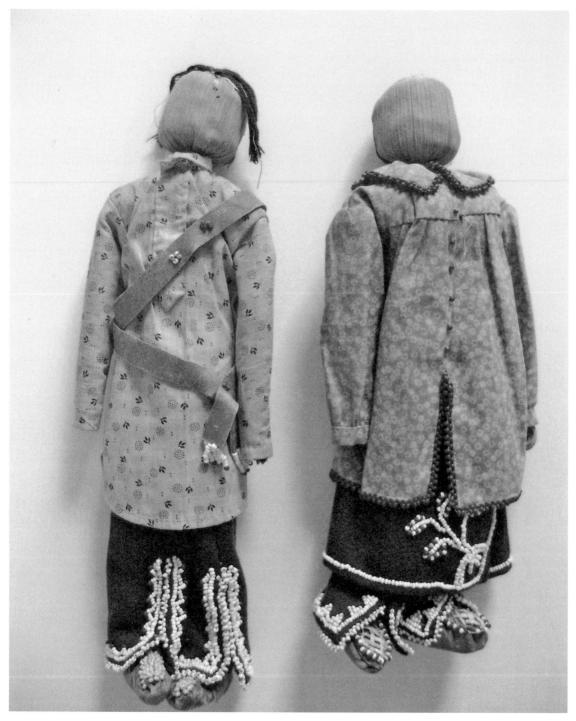

Pair of faceless Iroquois corn dolls. Edward Guarino collection, c. 1900.

The Iroquois tell the story of their mother goddess, Ataensic, who fell from the heavens because she had wanted a taste of earthly life and was caught mid-flight on the wings of birds, which gently dropped her onto the back of Grandmother Turtle. There she gave birth to twins, Hahgweh-daetgah the wicked and Hahgwehdiyu the good. When Ataensic died, the twins used her remains to create a world, but because of their constant conflicts, it was imperfect. From the divine body came corn, Hahgwe-hdiyu's gift to humanity. The young Cha-teaubriand visited the Iroquois in 1791 and cited their mythology in *Atala* (1801): "The Juggler invokes Michabou, genie of wa-ters. He tells of the wars of the great Hare against Matchi-Manitou, god of evil; he sings of the first man and of the beautiful Ataensic, who fell from the heavens for having lost their innocence, of the earth reddened by the blood of brothers." Every day in their prayers, the Iroquois thanked the Three Sisters, who brought them the resources essential for their lives: corn, beans, and squash.

Portrait of Nowadluk, an Inuit of Alaska, by the four Lomen brothers, who photographed Arctic life during the gold rush, 1903.

Iroquois women gave their daughters faceless dolls, telling them the story of Sister Corn. So excited to have been singled out as one of the supporters of life, Sister Corn went to ask her Creator what more she could do to please her people. The Creator had the idea of making a beautiful doll from corn husks, which he sent from the heavens to Iroquois children. The doll went from village to village. Everywhere people were amazed at her beauty, and so she became vain. The Cre-ator realized what had happened and put her in her place, threatening to punish her but without spelling out how. The doll nodded her head in agreement but only flaunted herself all the more. One day as she was walking near the water, she saw her reflection and could not help admiring herself, for in fact, she was very beau-tiful. It was then that the Creator sent a giant owl from the heavens. The owl stole the image of the doll's face out of the water. Since then, when an Iroquois mother gives a faceless doll to her child, she tells her this story. It is not right to believe you are better than someone else, since the Creator gave every creature a special talent. For those who follow Chateaubriand's trail in North America, these curious spec-ular dolls of the Iroquois tell a crucial tale.

The fusional attitude of the Amerindians toward their land is well known. Smohalla, one of the prophets of the ephemeral Ghost Dance religion, which ap-peared in the late nineteenth century, expressed it in these terms: "You ask me to plow the ground. Shall I take a knife and tear my mother's breast? Then when I die she will not take me to her bosom to rest. You ask me to dig for stone. Shall I dig under her skin for her bones? Then when I die I cannot enter her body to be born again. You ask me to cut grass and make hay and sell it and be rich like white men. But how dare I cut off my mother's hair."

Earth goddesses abound in Amerindian creation stories. The Cherokee trace their origin back to Selu, the Corn Mother, who tore open her chest to feed her people with the grains that came out of it. For the Pueblo Indians, the first mothers were Blue Corn Woman, mother of summer, and White Corn Maiden, mother of winter. The Apache claimed to descend from the Child of the Water, who was protected by his mother, the white-painted woman, so that he could kill all the monsters in this world and ensure peace.

RITUALS AND INITIATION

The story goes that in ancient times, when animals spoke to human beings, an old grandmother maintained good relations with Iktomi, a spider who had built an enormous web at the top of her tepee. Every time children paid a visit to the grandmother, she forbade them to touch the spiderweb. One day, Iktomi left the tepee and wanted to thank the grandmother for having protected her house for so long. "I give you my web as a gift," she told her, "for it will help you trap bad dreams. They will be caught in the center of my web and burned by the sun's rays. Add the feathers of birds, which connect the human world to the spirit world, and good dreams will come down to earth on feathers to help your people's dreamers." So it was that the Ojibwe and the Wyandot received from the ancestral spider their dreamcatchers, which guided them in life.

In their incessant rounds of rituals, the ancient North Americans exorcised conflicts by encouraging everyone to speak in a great theatrical performance by the entire community. The rich variety of rites and objects supporting their spiritual life has considerably enriched humanity's material and immaterial heritage.

The Amerindians of the Pacific Northwest carved totem poles, genealogical trees that towered over their villages. They also invented the "talking stick," which can be considered an instrument of indigenous democracy that provided sacred protection for the words of each community member in turn. Most Far West tribes devoutly transmitted across the ages their medicine bundles filled with relics. Wampum, belts woven by Iroquois women from porcupine quills and shells, were precious possessions. The Navajo were masters of the ephemeral: they composed colored sandpaintings, mandalas or rosettes, which organized their cosmos

Woman from Ontario with an owl, a familiarity lost with the vanishing of the totemic world, c. 1910.

Navajo sandpainting created
for the shaman's wind
ceremony. Photograph by
Edward S. Curtis, 1905.

Talking stick, still
used at gatherings.

Medicine bundles hold different relics from a life and are precious possessions within nonmaterialistic cultures. Here, the bags of a Piegan. Photograph by Edward S. Curtis, 1911.

Left: Drawing of kachina dolls by Jesse Walter Fewkes (1850–1930), an anthropologist who studied Hopi dances and rites, 1894.

Above: Edward S. Curtis was fascinated by the kachina dolls, here depicting Hopi dancers, 1905.

but were erased with the first breath. Their children still draw symbolic figures in the air with a string attached to their fingers. Some of the string games played by older children reproduce configurations of heavenly constellations. The Navajo dictionary compiled by the Franciscan fathers (1910) lists six original string games, each representing a different constellation. Among the Hopi and Zuni of the Southwest, kachinas are the spirits of rain, of fire, or of the snake, often mischievous pranksters who can be either beneficial or harmful. At ritual ceremonies, these kachina spirits are embodied by masked and costumed dancers. After the celebration, painted wooden dolls that meticulously depict each of the dancers are given to the children, so that they may become familiar with the spirit world. Since André Breton's time, these kachina dolls have become so highly prized by "first arts" collectors that the trade in them has recently given rise to protests by Native Americans, at Sotheby's, for example. Across the Americas, dances in masks and elaborate costumes were the driving force of indigenous religiosity. If we listen carefully, we can be sure that these peoples thrived on the celebration of life.

Amerindian religiosity did not separate spirituality from the rest of life. Women and men sought the aid of supernatural powers during solitary "vision quests" or at clan rites or tribal ceremonies. The vision quest—actually a plea for a vision—was the equivalent of a rebirth. Usually the young initiates went away by themselves for four days of prayer and fasting in the wild, so that the Great Spirit might grant them a vision to inspire their life.

One of the most important rituals, widespread on the North American continent, took place in a sweat lodge. This recurrent activity of purification was also a demonstration of strength and courage. Mourning Dove, or Hum-isha-ma, to give her Salish name, was born in a canoe in Idaho in 1884. The first published Amerindian woman writer, she describes the sweat lodge in her novel *Cogewea the Half-Blood: A Depiction of the Great Montana Cattle Range* (1927).

Elsewhere, she says: "The greatest of all deities among the tribes of North America was the sweat lodge. Its use was universal among the people of the forest, and many tribes still hold fast to its traditional sacredness. . . . During times of affliction or troubles in life, the Indian always turned to the sweat lodge to make a prayerful appeal. It was a place that made no distinctions. All could go there: rich or poor, weak or strong, simple-minded or great in knowledge. . . . All were equal to enter the lodge to pray and worship our Creator. There were no lines drawn between any of them: male or female, old or young. All had the same privileges to enter a church open to the public, regardless of race."

Other Native American women have also left accounts of such spiritual connections. Lucy Thompson, also called Che-na-wah Weitch-ah-wa (1856–1932), a Yurok grandmother living on the Klamath River in Northern California, published several copies of a book, *To the American Indian: Reminiscences of a Yurok Woman* (1916), in which she describes the initiation of women doctors by her people: "Women doctors are made and educated, which comes about in a very peculiar way. They are usually from the daughters of wealthy families. Most of them

Painted wooden kachina dolls brought back from the Brooklyn Museum's expedition to the southwestern United States in 1904. The fascination of "first arts" lovers for these Hopi dolls began at that time.

In search of a vision, two women shamans, a Naskoot (left) and
a Clayoquot (right), belonging to two Pacific Coast tribes versed
in totemism. Photographs by Edward S. Curtis, 1915.

begin quite young, and often the doctor will take one of her daughters that she
selects along with her and begin by teaching her to smoke and help her in her at-
tendance on the sick, and at the right time will commence with her at the sweathouse, while others will have a dream that they are doctors, and then the word
will be given out. And in either case along in the late fall all will be made ready,
the day being set. The sweathouse (which is the white man's name and does not
have the same meaning in our language; we call it Ur-girk) being selected, they
take her to it, dressed with a heavy skirt that comes down to her ankles and which
is made of the inner bark of the maple, with her arms and breast bare. They all go
into the sweathouse, there being from fifteen to twenty men and women in number, she having a brother or cousin, sometimes two, that look after her. All begin
to sing songs that are used for the occasion, dance jumping up and down, going
slowly around the fire and to the right. They keep this up until she is wet with per-
spiration, as wet as the water could make her, and when she gets so tired that she
can stand up no longer, one of her brothers or cousins takes her on his back with
her arms around his neck and keeps her going until she is completely exhausted.
Then they take her out and into the house. There she is bathed in warm water and
then allowed to sleep as long as she wishes, which revives her and gives her back
her strength. On awakening she appears rested and vigorous, with a beautiful

Frame of a Cheyenne sweat lodge. Photograph by Edward S. Curtis, 1910.

Navajo healing ceremony, during which the patient sweats
under a blanket while listening to sacred songs. Photograph
by Edward S. Curtis, c. 1905.

complexion. . . . Sometimes she will be from three to ten years before being ready for the final graduation exercises, when she will be taken back to some almost inaccessible place on a high peak or on a very high rock where they will smoke, pray and fast for three to five days." Thompson tells how the young woman "can bear hardships and punishment without complaint or murmur that would make a bear whine." Finally, she is awarded her diploma in front of her assembled peers, a scene that may well evoke medical students taking the Hippocratic oath. For Amerindians, women doctors were considered visionaries. They saw the cause of the pain and could extract it from the suffering body, in some cases by sucking it out and singing for hours.

SHE IS MAN'S FUTURE

Archie Fire Lame Deer and Wallace Black Elk point out that the Sioux religion is the only one in the world taught by a woman and intended for men. The sages of the Great Plains recount that long ago a beautiful young woman dressed in the hides of a young white bison appeared to two hunters. The younger of them, not knowing his manners, attempted to take her by force; a cloud descended upon him and turned him into a skeleton. The other was frightened and tried to flee, but the young woman told him she was the sister of all the men of his tribe and asked him to announce to them that she would be coming the next day. Having returned to the village, the man proclaimed the news, and the chief decided to receive the woman. In the early morning, she arrived from the west, introduced herself as the sister of them all, and entered the chief's tepee. From her bag the young woman drew a pipe disassembled into two pieces: the bowl, made of a red stone carved into the shape of a recumbent bison; and the wooden stem with eagle feathers hanging from it. She explained to the assembled tribe that the sacred pipe was a gift from Wakan Tanka to that people, who were not to smoke it except to ask for his assistance, since it was an important peace symbol. She told them that, by means of the pipe's smoke, their message would reach her, and she would transmit it to the Great Spirit. As the sun set, she departed toward the west whence she had come. As she got farther from the village and reached the horizon, she metamorphosed into a white bison. That earned her the nickname "White Bison Woman," and her pipe was called "Little Bison Pipe." As she left them, she said that

A Navajo mother and child. Photograph by William Pennington, c. 1920.

Far left: Clayoquot shaman with her traditional cloak woven from cedar wood fiber. Photograph by Edward S. Curtis, 1915.

Left: Peace pipe bags are some of the most elaborate objects. Photograph by Edward S. Curtis, 1908.

Opposite: In anticipation of a ceremony, peace pipes lie in the medicine lodge of an Arikara wise man. Photograph by Edward S. Curtis, 1908.

she would return to earth at the end of four cycles, upon the collapse of the bison who prevents the catastrophes threatening the world. That bison loses a strand of hair every year and a hoof every cycle; he is now almost bald and stands on only one foot. Black Elk, the Sioux Marcel Proust, said that the sweet grass burning in his pipe was the hair of Mother Earth and that, when the spirit of his grandmother returned, it brought with it that smell, that fragrance. The young White Bison Woman, the magic woman of the Far West, gave men the peace pipe ceremony, so that they would see to the heart of the human presence on earth. As for women, their power as clairvoyants and healers is so great that they take no heed of the rite.

In the 1920s Susan Bordeaux Bettelyoun (1857–1945), daughter of a French trapper father and a Lakota mother, recounted the story of her life to historian Josephine Waggoner. Their book, *With My Own Eyes,* bears witness to the ravaged life of her people during her era, while at the same time relaying the voices of the elders. Bettelyoun evokes what the ritual of the peace pipe represented, even for those who did not smoke it: "The peace pipe was considered such a sacred pact that no one ever broke its laws. If they did, they came to grief brought on by their own untruthfulness, for breaking the law of truth. All that was unclean was never practiced with the peace pipe. The white people, little understanding the power of the pipe as something sacred and holy, doubted the veracity of the peace made with the peace pipe. It is often laughed and jested about by them. The peace pipe, like the white man's sacrament, was a symbol of truth and inward grace; its laws were spiritual and not to be desecrated." The ritualized pastimes of the ancient Amerindians connected them to the Great Spirit.

WOMEN'S TEACHINGS

The biographies of Amerindian women attest to the importance of grandmothers in rites of passage and spiritual initiation. Songs, tales, and legends were transmitted by the grandmothers until far into the night.

Beverly Hungry Wolf writes: "One of the finest rewards for being an old woman comes from going outside the camp circle early each morning, to face the rising sun and call out the names of all the children, grandchildren, great-grandchildren, and friends, during a prayer that shows the old woman's thankfulness and humbleness before the Creator, and brings cheerful tears into the eyes of all those in the camp who can hear." Born in 1950 on the Kainai, or Blood, reservation in Canada, Hungry Wolf was raised in the language and customs of her Blackfoot tribe. At school, she discovered modern civilization and a way of life that was eclipsing her cultural heritage. After studies and travels, she returned to her school as a teacher. Distressed at seeing the traditions of her people disappearing, Hungry Wolf devoted her time to collecting the memories of her mother, grandmother, and other women of the tribe and reconstituting the values of the Blackfoot culture in books such as *The Ways of My Grandmothers*.

Luther Standing Bear (1868–1939), raised in the oral tradition, then educated within mainstream American culture, is one of few in his generation able to make a substantial contribution to the history of his people. In *Land of the Spotted Eagle* (1933), he recalls: "Grandmother filled a place that mother did not fill, and the older she got the more, it seemed, we children depended upon her for attention. I can never forget one of my grandmothers, mother's mother, and what wonderful care she took of me. As a story-teller, she was a delight not only to me but

Opposite: Native American mother and child. Photograph from the Whyte Museum collections, c. 1900.

Right: Navajo woman transporting a well-swaddled baby. Photograph by William Pennington, c. 1920.

Ojibwe mother and her papoose. Photograph by Roland W. Reed, 1908.

Right: Portrait of an elderly Plains Indian woman. Photograph by Richard Throssel, 1910.

Below: Apache woman and her child, 1886.

to other little folks of the village. Her sense of humor was keen and she laughed as readily as we. . . . Then grandmother, with the help of grandfather, was our teacher. When grandfather sang his songs, she encouraged us to dance to them. She beat time with him and showed us how to step with his tunes. Seldom did she go walking in the woods or on the plains without taking us with her, and these hours were profitable ones in knowledge, for scarcely a word or an act was not filled with the wisdom of her life."

Standing Bear also reports a few principles of Sioux education: "The Indian mother . . . taught her boy honesty, fearlessness, and duty, and her girl industry, loyalty, and fidelity. Into the character of babes and children mother-strength left the essence of strong manhood and womanhood. Every son was taught to be generous to the point of sacrifice, truthful no matter what the cost, and brave to the point of death. These impulses—generosity, truthfulness, and bravery—may be dressed and polished in schools and universities, but their fundamental nature is never touched. After childhood days, mothers still could not forsake the part of guide and teacher—for youth, as well as childhood, must be directed, and there

Opposite: Inuit mother photographed in the studio that the Lomen brothers set up in the American El Dorado of Alaska, 1903.

Above: Crow camp, between sky and water. Photograph by Richard Throssel, 1910.

was no substitute. So Lakota mothers taught youth how to worship and pray, how to know mercy and kindness, and how to seek right and justice."

Charles Eastman (1858–1939) is another Sioux who speaks of the women in his life. A doctor and writer, he penned many texts on the history of his people, some of which are collected in *Light on the Indian World: The Essential Writings of Charles Eastman (Ohiyesu)* (2002) and *Living in Two Worlds* (2012). He evokes the figure of the Amerindian woman:

"The average white man still believes that the Indian woman of the old days was little more than a beast of burden to her husband. But the missionary who has lived among his people, the sympathetic observer of their everyday life, holds a very different opinion. You may generally see the mother and her babe folded close in her own shawl, indicating the real and most important business of her existence. Without the child, life is but a hollow play, and all Indians pity the couple who are unable to obey the primary command, the first law of real happiness. . . .

The Indian woman has always been the silent but telling power behind life's activities. At the same time she shared equally with her mate in the arduous duties of primitive society. Possessed of true feminine dignity and modesty, she was expected to be his equal in physical endurance and skill, but his superior in spiritual insight. She was looked to for the endowment of her child with nature's gifts and powers. . . . The Indian mother was the spiritual teacher of the child, as well as its tender nurse, and she brought its developing soul before the 'Great Mystery' as soon as she was aware of its coming. At the age of five to eight years, she turned her boy over to his father for manly training, and to the grandparents for traditional instruction, but the girl child remained under her close and thoughtful supervision. She preserved man from soul-killing materialism by herself owning what few possessions they had."

NOSTALGIA

The field of Amerindian ethnology has a peculiarity unknown to those who study Africa, Asia, and Oceania: historical accounts and biographies of women abound. The human sciences have felt the impact of the "hidden half" of humanity earlier in North America. Our vision broadens to include the unknown female continent.

In the early twentieth century, the American Museum of Natural History sent a few anthropologists on a mission to collect information about the last survivors of vanishing tribes. Gilbert L. Wilson (1869–1930) spent ten years among the Hidatsa on their reservation in Fort Berthold, North Dakota. His book, *Waheenee: An Indian Girl's Story* (1982), is told in the words of Waheenee, a tribal elder: "I was born in an earth lodge by the mouth of the Knife river, in what is now North Dakota, three years after the smallpox winter. . . . I am an old woman now. The buffaloes and black-tail deer are gone, and our Indian ways are almost gone. Sometimes I find it hard to believe that I ever lived them. My little son grew up in the white man's school. He can read books, and he owns cattle and has a farm. He is a leader among our Hidatsa people, helping teach them to follow the white man's road. He is kind to me. We no longer live in an earth lodge, but in a house with chimneys; and my son's wife cooks by a stove. But for me, I cannot forget our old ways. Often in summer I rise at daybreak and steal out to the cornfields; and as I hoe the corn I sing to it, as we did when I was young. No one cares for our corn songs now. Sometimes at evening I sit, looking out on the big Missouri. The sun sets, and dusk steals over the water. In the shadows I seem again to see our Indian village, with smoke curling upward from the earth lodges; and in the river's roar I hear the yells of the warriors, the laughter of little children as of old. It is but an old woman's dream. Again I see but shadows and hear only the roar of the river; and tears come into my eyes. Our Indian life, I know, is gone forever."

In *To the American Indian: Reminiscences of a Yurok Woman,* Lucy Thompson, a Yurok grandmother from California, proclaims her intention to transmit the truth of her culture: "As there has been so much said and written about the

Chinook elder with basket contemplates the Pacific Ocean.
Photograph by Edward S. Curtis, 1912.

American Indians, with my tribe, the Klamath Indians, included, by the white people, which is guessed at and not facts . . . in this book I will endeavor to tell all in a plain and truthful way, without the least coloring of the facts." Some 150 years have passed since Thompson and her people witnessed the gold rush, when prospectors from the East arrived to scrape together their fortune from the last gold deposits in the West. After the miners had left, other fields opened up for anthropologists, linguists, historians, and folklorists. Library shelves bear witness to their studies, but it is also heartening to read indigenous versions of history.

In the 1940s Ella Deloria wrote the novel *Waterlily,* which was published in 1989, seventeen years after her death. It is a rare contribution to our understanding of women's status in Sioux culture by one of its own people. In 1952 Deloria wrote to an editor in the hope of publishing her novel: "This may sound a little naïve, Mr. Beebe, but I actually feel that I have a mission: To make the Dakota people understandable, as human beings, to the white people who have to deal with them. I feel that one of the reasons for the lagging advancement of the Dakotas has been that those who came out among them to teach and preach, went on the assumption that the Dakotas had *nothing,* no rules of life, no social organization, no ideals. And they tried to pour white culture into, as it were, a vacuum, and when that did not work out, because it is not a vacuum after all, they concluded that the Indians were impossible to change and train. What they should have done first, before daring to start their program, was to study everything possible of Dakota life, and see what made it go, in the old days, and what was still so deeply rooted that it could not be rudely displaced without some hurt. . . . I feel that I have this work cut out for me and if I do not make all I know available before I die, I will have failed by so much." There is no better way to set out the terms of the debate about identity, particularism, and minorities. To listen is to travel half the road toward a greater understanding of reality.

Opposite: Ponemah, a fierce-looking young Ojibwe. Photograph by Roland W. Reed, 1908.

3

First Encounters with the Spanish

Are they not men? Have they not reason and a soul? Are you not bound to love them as yourselves?

—Bartolomé de las Casas (1484–1566),
A Short Account of the Destruction of the Indies (1542)

Just imagine Christopher Columbus (1451–1506) and his crew landing on the beach of the Bahamas one fine morning in October 1492, facing the unknown—a magical moment, an early close encounter of the third kind. Shadows move among the trees, human silhouettes appear. The New World emerges to stare at the Old, which has come seeking it. Do they embrace? Do they look each other over? Do they laugh and speak? The ignorance on both sides is commensurate with the sudden revelation entailed by the encounter. The envoys of Isabella the Catholic took the measure of the Taino, who responded in kind. Each sought in the other's eyes connivance or equivalence, a sign of wickedness or innocence. If we are to get a sense of the terror and wonder of that encounter, we must go back to our own childhood years on the playground, where affinities and enmities at the start of the year turned on a look or a gesture. The Taino identified their island as "Guanahani." Columbus, "Admiral of the Ocean Sea," immediately renamed it "San Salvador."

Above: Hernán Cortés and La Malinche, the Totonac woman who served as the Spaniards' guide. Nineteenth-century engraving.

82

The arrival of Amerigo Vespucci
on the South American continent
in 1499. Engraving by Théodore de
Bry, from *Les Grands Voyages*, 1618.

Christopher Columbus
encounters an indige-
nous woman. Fresco by
Constantino Brumidi,
Rotunda of the Capitol,
Washington, DC, 1875.

GOLD AND DOMINION

In his letter of October 12, 1492, Columbus wrote to Luis de Santángel (d. 1498), finance minister to the court of Spain and his chief supporter: "At daybreak, a great multitude of men assembled on the bank, all young and well built, with attractive faces. Their hair is not curly but free and thick like horses' manes. They have the biggest foreheads I have ever seen. Their eyes are large and very beautiful. These men are not black but the same color as the inhabitants of the Canary Islands." Then came the moment of the Columbian exchange that would transform the world: "So that they would develop friendly dispositions toward us, because I knew they were people who could be converted to our Holy Faith by love rather than by force, I gave them a few red caps and glass beads, which they put around their necks, as well as other trinkets, which gave them great pleasure. They go about as naked as the day they were born, even the women, though I was able to see only a very young girl. What I did see were young men under thirty . . . who ought to make good and very skillful servants, to judge by how diligently they repeat what is said to them." True to the logic of his quest, the "discoverer" of America was looking for King Solomon's mines: "I observed them very attentively to learn whether they had gold. Upon seeing the little gold rings hanging from their noses, I ascertained through sign language that, to the south, on the other side of the island, there is a king who possesses large pots of gold."

Columbus, noting the absence of metal weapons among the "Indians" (as he too hastily called them), adds: "I will be able to vanquish them all with fifty men and to rule them as I see fit." The Spaniards' breastplates, halberds, and fire-arms would assure them the "mechanical victories" of which Montaigne (1533–1592) speaks. Columbus then encountered hostile Ciguayo, resistant to his demands: the first scuffle on the journey to what is now the Dominican Republic followed. These "docile servants" were quickly transformed into horrible "cannibals." The Spaniards took some twenty prisoners, seven or eight of whom would reach Seville alive and cause a sensation.

On September 25, 1493, Columbus left Cádiz for his second journey, at the command of seventeen ships and twelve hundred crewmen, soldiers, priests, and farmers, to found the colony of New Spain. Michele da Cuneo was on board. That Italian adventurer and childhood friend of Columbus left behind the first

An Arawak woman with a parrot, as she appeared to the conquistadores. Engraving from John Gabriel Stedman's accounts, 1792.

An old cannibal woman offers fruit to the conquistadores.
Engraving from Théodore de Bry's *Grands Voyages*, 1590.

narrative of an encounter between a European man and an Amerindian woman. His letter, written on October 28, 1495, tells how he and his men attacked a band of Carib Indians: "We captured a canoe with all its men, whom we are sending to Spain as slaves. After returning to the ship, I chose a beautiful cannibal girl, and the admiral gave her to me. Having led her, naked as is their custom, to my quarters, I attempted to take my pleasure in her. When I tried to have my way with her, she refused and scratched me with her nails so hard that I was sorry I had begun. Then, seeing how things were going, I took a rope and thrashed her so thoroughly that she screamed as you would not believe. In the end, let me tell you, we got on so well that I had the impression she had studied at a school for whores." That awful story of rape, recounted as a macho conquest, boded ill for future relations between the Spanish imperial forces and Amerindian women.

In February 1495, Columbus took 1,500 Taino prisoner in Haiti. Onto his ships he loaded 550 of them, whom he would sell as slaves in the Mediterranean.

Español con India.
Mestiza.

Mestizo con Española.
Castizo.

Castizo con Española.
Español.

Español con Negra.
Mulato.

5
Mulato con Española.
Morisco.

6
Morisco con Española.
Chino.

7
Chino con India.
Salta atras.

Salta atras con Mulata.
Lobo.

9
Lobo con China.
Gibaro.

1o
Gibaro con Mulata
Albarazado

11
Albarazado con Negra
Canbujo.

12
Canbujo con India.
Sanbaigo.

13
Sanbaigo con Loba
Calpamulato.

14
Calpamulato con Canbuja.
Tente en el Aire.

15
Tente en el Aire con Mulata
Note entiendo.

16
Note entiendo con India.
Torna atras.

Cuneo noted: "Among them were many women with small children at their breasts. In their efforts to escape us, these mothers, frightened that we were pursuing them, left their children on the ground and fled like madwomen." Thus it was that Columbus himself inaugurated the transatlantic slave trade—but in the opposite direction. And it was Cortés, conqueror of Mexico, who began the African slave trade, placing an order with Genoa merchants for five hundred for his Mexican plantations, thereby circumventing the 1542 ban by Charles V (1500–1558) on enslaving the indigenous population.

BODIES AND SOULS

At first, the Europeans doubted the very humanity of the indigenous people they encountered. Because they did not fit in with the standard understanding of the realm of Christendom of the times, it was thought that perhaps they did not count and could reasonably be enslaved by their western conquerors. It was not until the famous Valladolid debate that the bull *Sublimis Deus* (1537) by Pope Paul III (1468–1549) settled the question: Indians were "truly men" and creatures of God, capable of receiving the Gospel.

   While that discourse on abstract ideals was underway, Amerindian women were already demonstrating the truth biologically by bearing viable offspring. The terminology applied to these children is telling: *mulatto* comes from the term "mule," for the generally sterile interspecies cross between a horse and a donkey. Having set off to satisfy their hunger for gold, the fearless conquerors found more immediate gratification with indigenous women whom they did not hesitate to force themselves on, as illustrated by Cuneo's account.

Opposite: Casta painting from New Spain showing sixteen combinations of races and their classification. Oil, eighteenth century.

Right: Under the influence of La Malinche, the Indians take Cortés as their leader. Lithograph.

Cortés reaches Moctezuma II, leader of the Aztec Empire. Sixteenth-century Mexican illumination.

Florentine navigator Amerigo Vespucci (1454–1512), after whom the Americas are named, noted in his letters that Indians of both sexes went about without modesty or shame. Of the women, he wrote: "They are very fertile and do not avoid working when they are pregnant." He told how he had seen Indian mothers slip away briefly into the woods to give birth, then calmly return to their fieldwork or to the tanning of hides. That marked the genesis of one of the clichés about Amerindian women that would long be perpetuated, including by Hollywood. Another cliché concerns their sexual hospitality. It may have been considered an affront to the indigenous people for a woman they were offering to be rejected, as the Europeans remarked incredulously. But perhaps this should be seen instead as an expression of the imperative for exogamy? Everything depends on one's point of view. These descriptions and images, which began to circulate with the spread of printed matter, would long influence the European view of American "savages."

If the "Columbus theory" of the origin of syphilis turns out to be true, it would be an interesting counterpoint to the introduction of devastating old-world diseases in the Americas. According to this account, sailors on the first transatlantic voyage brought back from the New World *Treponema pallidum*, the bacterium that causes syphilis. And when several members of the crew from Columbus's first journey joined the Holy League of Venice against King Charles VIII (1470–1498) and his war with Italy, the sexually transmitted disease was disseminated throughout Europe, with an estimated death toll of five million. The infamous "Neapolitan disease" became a great pox that terrorized Europe for five centuries.

Nevertheless, the question of sexual relations between Amerindians, Europeans, and Africans is a complex subject barely touched on by historians. And yet, with Columbus's arrival, European men and Amerindian women intermingled. One of the oldest reported cases was that of Gonzalo Guerrero, a Spaniard shipwrecked on the coast of the Yucatán, and a Maya noblewoman, with whom he had three children. We may assume that he was not the first man to arrive on the horizon and father children. The colossal stone statues of heads with African features, left by the pre-Columbian Olmec civilization in the Isthmus of Tehuantepec, have long posed a challenge to historians and engendered theories of earlier arrivals from other shores.

The relationship of Hernán Cortés and La Malinche (c. 1499/1505–1529) is the best known example. Cortés formed an alliance with the Totonac, enemies of the Aztec, in order to attack the empire. He chose La Malinche from among twenty slaves, making her his concubine, interpreter, adviser, and guide. Also called "Malintzin" and baptized Doña Marina by the conquistadores from beyond the sea, she has usually been considered the willing victim and principal agent of the Spanish conquest of Mexico. Whether victim or traitor, it was she who told Cortés of a great king named Moctezuma II (1466–1520) living in a fabulous city in the clouds and who confided that he had thirty kings as his vassals, and they all hated him and would form an alliance with the man who could prove more powerful than the Aztec Empire. It was also La Malinche who whispered to the conquistador that he could take advantage of the Mexican myth of Quetzalcoatl by passing himself off as the envoy of the "God who must one day return."

When Cortés captured Tenochtitlan after a bloody siege, on November 8, 1519, and Moctezuma II fell permanently silent, La Malinche carried on as the

The first encounter between Cortés and Moctezuma II in Tenochtitlan, November 8, 1519. Lithograph, c. 1890.

La Malinche helps Cortés subjugate the Aztecs.
Mural painting by Roberto Cueva del Río, 1952.

voice of the mediator and lover who bore the first mestizo child of the Americas, a child who spoke a new language, Castilian. That son, Martin Cortés (c. 1523–c. 1595), known as El Mestizo, was sent as a page to the Spanish court of King Philip II (1527–1598). In the preface to his translation of *Relación de las ceremonias y ritos y población y gobierno de los indios de la Provincia de Michoacán*, J. M. G. Le Clézio reminds us that the Spaniards called the Purépecha of Michoacán "Tarascos," that is, "fathers-in-law," ridiculing them for the women the Spaniards had taken from them.

THE BALLAD OF NEW SPAIN

In the decade following Cortés's epic conquest in Mexico, Pedro de Heredia (d. 1554) seized Colombia using the same expedients. Thanks to the assistance of India Catalina (1495–1529), a young woman from the Calamari tribe whom he had captured and who served as his guide, this conquistador subjugated the local population. India Catalina is now portrayed in Colombia as the peaceful mediator between Spanish troops and the indigenous peoples. Like La Malinche, she is a contradictory figure: the sheltering mother of the mestizos but also a traitor and whore.

Princess Tecuichpotzin (c. 1509–1550), known to history as Isabel Moctezuma, was just as important as La Malinche for the conquest of the New World

Above: A fantasy welcome into the New World's boudoir. Engraving by Nicolas-Eustache Maurin, nineteenth century.

Left: Encounters between Spanish men and Indian women produced mestizos. Painting by Juan Rodríguez Juárez, 1720.

Europe supported by Africa & America.

Opposite: Europe (in the center), supported by Africa and America, leads the dance. Engraving by William Blake, from John Gabriel Stedman's accounts, 1792.

Above: Native American cooking. Engraving from Théodore de Bry's *Grands Voyages,* after a painting by John White, 1590.

and the racial intermingling that followed. The daughter of Moctezuma II, she was married at the age of twelve to the last emperor, Cuauhtémoc, who was hanged by the Spanish in 1525. She was therefore the legitimate heir to the Aztec Empire. Cortés would make her a symbol of the continuity of rule. She converted to Catholicism in 1528 and was given in marriage by Cortés to his close friend Alonso de Grado (1494–1527), who died soon thereafter. Cortés then took her in and impregnated her instead. Their daughter Leonor (1528–?) would inherit her share of the realm. Isabel later married Juan Cano de Saavedra (1502–1572), with whom she had three sons and two daughters. The couple became Spanish grandees in 1766, and the Palacio Cano Moctezuma can still be seen in Cáceres, Extremadura.

According to the Spanish chronicles, Moctezuma II was the father of about a hundred children, and fifty of his concubines were pregnant when the Spaniards invaded. His prolific line continues on both sides of the Atlantic. Several of his heirs were acknowledged by the Spanish crown and granted noble titles. One of Moctezuma II's daughters, Xipaguacin, married Juan de Grau, baron of

Atlas cartouche illustrating Vespucci's discovery of the new American continent.
Engraving by Theodor Galle, c. 1630.

Toleriu, an officer under Cortés who took her to Spain with his Mexican court. She
died in Andorra in 1537. There are still many descendants of the house of Grau-
Moctezuma in that corner of the Pyrenees. The genealogical tree of Moctezuma
II's children is instructive: in following the trail of the marriages between Spanish and Mexican elites from the beginning, we see clearly the process by which the
victors repeatedly took control through marriage with the vanquished—as they
converted to become good Catholics, of course.

The new religion introduced by the conquerors would also give the New
World orphans a spiritual mother to revere. In 1531, at a site dedicated to the Aztec goddess Tonantzin, the Virgin of Guadalupe appeared to a simple porter. She
would console the Indian people, and the image of the sacrificed Christ replaced
that of Quetzalcoatl, the immolated god. For all these reasons combined, Mexican
syncretism better accepted its *mestizaje* than would be the case farther north.

At the start of the Spanish conquest, the royal couple, Ferdinand and Isabella, favored interethnic marriages in New Spain, which gave them a more solid
base of power and hastened the Indians' assimilation. But the rise of mestizos
soon began to worry the Council of the Indies, which stripped that population

of its class standing through a series of discriminatory laws from 1550 onward. The rebellion of the mestizos and Creoles against the Spanish authorities in 1565 marked the birth of Mexican national feeling.

ORIGINAL IMAGERY

On the new atlases of the world produced in this era, a cartouche appeared in the western zone depicting America as a naked woman in a bucolic setting *à l'antique*. The first engravings of the New World were printed by Rhineland Protestants and would spread the "dark legend" of the gold-hungry Spanish conquistadores throughout Europe. A century after Columbus's discovery, *Les Grands Voyages* (1585–1634), a series of books by Théodore de Bry (1528–1598), for the first time offered the reading public a vast panorama of the European conquests in the Americas and the first contacts with Amerindians. The volume devoted to New Spain shows indigenous peoples in their pre-Columbian paradise, followed by their subjugation by the Spaniards, who appear more diabolical than the so-called

An abundance of wonders in the New World: Vespucci arrives on the Island of Giants. Engraving from Théodore de Bry's *Grands Voyages*, 1602.

"savages." The engraving that represents Vasco Núñez de Balboa (1475–1519), who discovered the Pacific Ocean in 1513, as he contemplates his war dogs attacking natives accused of sodomy, would mark a historical milestone. De Bry also published selected passages from Bartolomé de las Casas's defense of the Indians, *A Short Account of the Destruction of the Indies*, which he illustrated with anti-Spanish engravings highlighting the slavery, torture, and cruelty practiced by the conquistadores.

Each volume of *Voyages* relates real historical events, stringing together accounts of explorers such as Antonio Pigafetta, Magellan's chronicler, and scholarly texts, for example: *A Briefe and True Report of the New Found Land of Virginia*, by the geographer and astronomer Thomas Harriot (1560–1621); *Historia natural y moral de las Indias*) (*Natural and Moral History of the Indies*, 1598), by the Jesuit naturalist José de Acosta (1539–1600), who tried his hand at classifying the various indigenous peoples; and *The Principal Navigations*, the navigation logs of the Virginia Company. But at the same time, *Les Grands Voyages* sensationalized that never-before-seen, never-before-heard-of world in imagery that abounds in representations of monsters with heads in the middle of their chests, giant Amazon women, and gothic dragons—a baroque mix of real people and prodigious creatures, of golden showers in El Dorado and cannibal sabbaths where women with pendulous breasts dance around an infernal cauldron, shaking scalps. Both the Bible and the mythology of antiquity provided the format for European artists of the Renaissance.

These artists had the greatest difficulty capturing the features of the New World's indigenous peoples, whom they had rarely seen in the flesh. The nude *à l'antique* became the obligatory frame of reference. Their Indians looked more like chubby Apollos or fleshy Dianas than the rugged peoples from the Siberian tundra who are supposedly their ancestors. In 1520, however, the artist Albrecht Dürer (1471–1528) expressed his admiration for Mexican objects he had glimpsed in Brussels: "In my whole life I have never seen anything that so delighted my heart, for I saw marvelous works of art there, and I was in raptures before the subtle genius of men of foreign lands." After all, artists are humanists.

In contrast, the volume of *Les Grands Voyages* devoted to the English colony of Virginia, which is more indulgent toward the Protestant colonists than toward their Spanish counterparts, tells the story of Pocahontas (c. 1595–1617), relying on the account of Captain John Smith (1580–1631). De Bry, who had never set foot in the Americas, was inspired primarily by the watercolors of John White (1540–1593), a talented artist whom he freely lifted imagery from. White, cartographer for Sir Walter Raleigh (1552–1618) and Sir Richard Grenville (1542–1591) in their world travels, was also the governor of the "lost colony" of Roanoke Island, Virginia, England's first, short-

A land Sort to the Seuages esteeme aboue all other Torts

The turtle, one of the many specimens of North American fauna illustrated by John White, 1570–93.

Two Piegan women looking out at the horizon. Photograph by Edward S. Curtis, 1910.

lived attempt in 1585 to settle North America. The seventy paintings by White held at the British Museum, exhibited for the first time in 2007, constitute a unique documentation of the life of Algonquian societies in the sixteenth century. White was the first to draw Amerindians from life, depicting scenes of hunting and fishing, life in wigwams, festivities, dances and games, and religious rituals. Some illustrations show subsistence techniques such as slash-and-burn farming, the smoking of meat, and the fabrication of canoes from tree trunks, as well as specimens of North American flora and fauna. These images and their documentary value are witness to a tremendous human curiosity, in contrast to the brutality of mercenary encounters at that time.

The British would be more concerned than the Spaniards with their image, observing all forms of civility, sending an emissary from the governor of Jamestown to ask for the hand of the famous Pocahontas in marriage. That, at least, is what the conventional propaganda asserts. In reality, the New England Puritans would very quickly set up a segregationist society that would slow the process of racial mixing, but without ending it altogether. If Claude Lévi-Strauss had taken apart the Pocahontas myth, he would have had the chance to quote his beloved Montaigne: when the human race discovers a division of the world, nearly equal in greatness to that we knew before . . . every one gives the title of barbarism to everything that is not in use in his own country.

4

First Encounters with the English

SEVENTEENTH CENTURY: POCAHONTAS AND VIRGINIA

On May 14, 1607, three ships from the Virginia Company of London cast anchor in the Chesapeake Bay, an insalubrious place infested with mosquitoes and shunned by the indigenous people. Aboard were five hundred gentlemen and their servants, most wholly unacquainted with rural life, who had resolved to cross the Atlantic and found the first permanent English colony in North America, to be named Jamestown after the king of England. Left to the mercy of God, they arrived too late in the year to plant crops and had no reserves to get through the winter. Tens of thousands of Algonquian speakers had been living in the area for centuries, and thirty of the tribes had formed a chiefdom under the leadership of the great sachem Powhatan. At first, the indigenous people welcomed the new arrivals, organizing incessant festivities and tobacco ceremonies. They also gave the settlers bags of corn, a grain unknown to the English but crucial for their survival. In spite of that, at the end of the winter of 1609–10, only sixty-one of the colonists had lived through the famine. Archaeologists

Pocahontas would become an icon of popular culture.

Top: A packet of tobacco showing Pocahontas coming to John Smith's assistance, c. 1860.

Left: Chewing tobacco packaging bearing the effigy of the famous woman, 1868.

Opposite: An allegory of the New World portraying America in "native finery," depicted by Jules-Antoine Vauthier, 1820.

at the Smithsonian have recently brought to light instances of cannibalism in Jamestown, the oldest American colony. Such is the setting for the golden legend of an Indian princess.

Although her real name was Matoaka, she is better known as Pocahontas, which means "naughty, spoiled little girl." She was one of the many daughters of the powerful chief Powhatan (c. 1547–1618). Born in about 1595, she probably saw Europeans for the first time in 1607, when the English landed in Jamestown. The story of the first meeting between Pocahontas and Captain John Smith is the stuff of fiction. On December 29, 1607, Smith was leading a hunting party when he was taken prisoner by the Amerindians. According to him, he was at first welcomed by the great chief, who gave a feast in his honor, but was then abruptly pinned down on two large flat stones by warriors ready to immolate him. Suddenly a young woman threw herself on Smith and took his head in her arms, lying on top of his body to protect him. Pocahontas—for it was she—then stood up and pleaded for his safety. Chief Powhatan announced that he and Captain Smith were now friends and that he was adopting the Englishman as his son. Anthropologists have expressed doubts about this story. According to some, Pocahontas's gesture may have been part of a traditional ritual of execution and rescue that Smith did not understand. Nevertheless, the happy ending did not fail to attract Hollywood's notice: Disney's saccharine story obscures the ferocity of the first contacts, while playing to an American psyche hungry for romance. But the lovely story of Pocahontas continues. The playful child became Smith's friend and often visited him in Jamestown. It is said she turned cartwheels with the colonists' children to get closer to the settlers through her acrobatics. She also carried messages from her father, accompanied by warriors who came to exchange furs for copper and trinkets. In 1609 Smith was wounded in a gunpowder explosion and forced to

Dance of the Algonquin. Drawing by John White, 1590.

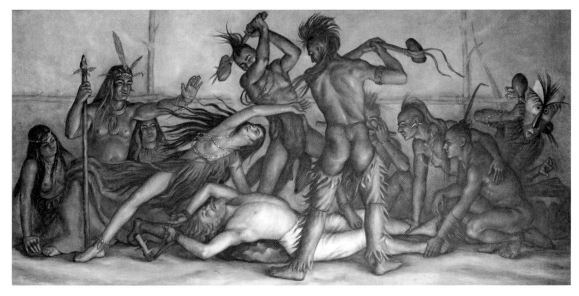

The persistence of a myth: Pocahontas saving the life of John Smith as painted by
Paul Cadmus to decorate the Court House Annex in Richmond, Virginia, 1939.

return to England. When Pocahontas inquired about her friend, she was told that
Smith had died.

The life of the mischievous Pocahontas then took a different turn. She was
kidnapped from her village along the banks of the Potomac by colonists who
sought to exchange her for several English prisoners held by Powhatan. For a
year, Pocahontas was confined to another colony known as Henricus, where she
learned English customs and the Christian religion. She was baptized under the
name Rebecca and later met John Rolfe (1585–1622), a devout tobacco farmer who
fell in love with her. The wedding took place in 1614; it was the first interracial
marriage in North American history. The couple had a child, Thomas Rolfe (1615–
1680). Pocahontas's marriage and her conversion to Christianity ushered in a period of peaceful relations between the local tribes and the colonists.

The first North American monoculture crop to be exported was tobacco,
not a basic necessity, though at the time people spoke of "tobacco-drinking." The
phenomenal success of Virginia tobacco resulted in a high demand for the product
in Europe. English ships cast anchor in the port of Jamestown and loaded up bar-
relfuls of rolled tobacco leaves. The Jamestown colonists quickly repaid their im-
migration debts by means of the little packets of tobacco sold in London. To attract
new investors to Virginia, the colony's plantation owners sent Rolfe to promote
Nicotiana tabacum among the Europeans. He would be accompanied by his wife,
thus assuring potential investors that the indigenous peoples of the New World
did not represent a threat. In 1616 the Rolfes sailed for England, along with a group
of eleven Native Americans. Pocahontas learned that John Smith was still alive
in London. The letter he wrote to Queen Anne (1574–1619) still survives: in it he

One of the first images of the indigenous peoples of the New World: a Secotan mother and her child. Drawing by John White, 1580.

asks the queen to make sure that Pocahontas is treated with the same respect as a royal visitor and not like a carnival freak. Pocahontas and Rolfe lived in London for a few months; according to Smith, who paid them a visit, Pocahontas called her husband "Sugar Daddy." In March 1617 the two set off on their return trip to Virginia. Along the way, the young woman fell sick and died shortly thereafter.

Although the life of Pocahontas symbolizes the warmth and connections between people of all backgrounds, in Virginia relations between the colonists and indigenous tribes rapidly festered. Those who were spared from the quarrels related to bartering and the violence that followed perished from smallpox or typhus. By 1611 the Paspahegh, the first tribe to be in contact with the colonists, had entirely vanished. Men were dying, but women were becoming even rarer, both among the locals and in the new Jamestown colony. In 1619 a first convoy of ninety young single women in search of husbands arrived from England. Until the end of the seventeenth century, many of these "tobacco brides," purchased for 150 pounds of tobacco—the price of their crossing paid by the company and a trousseau bestowed on them for their trouble—traveled to the colony with that aim in mind. A little later, the New France settlement would use the same expedients. Between 1663 and 1673, nearly eight hundred "King's Daughters," often orphans provided for at the sovereign's expense, were sent to Quebec to marry colonists.

An iconic moment in North American history: the First Thanksgiving, shared by the settlers and the Amerindians in a gesture of friendship and alliance. Painting by Jean Leon Gerome Ferris, c. 1920.

THE MAYFLOWER
AND NEW ENGLAND

On November 21, 1620, colonists of a different sort cast anchor to the north of Jamestown in Cape Cod Bay. The 102 pilgrims aboard the *Mayflower* (seventy-four men, eighteen women accompanying their husbands, seven young women with their parents, and three women traveling alone), along with the fifty crewmen, arrived in North America to found the biblical "city on a hill." These Puritan pioneers were no better adapted to survival in the woods than the Jamestown colonists had been. Those who did not starve to death were saved by the baskets of corn and bean offerings they discovered while digging through Amerindian burial mounds. For the first few months, the indigenous peoples did not show themselves. Muskets held off the arrows. The men went ashore to build cob huts, while the women remained confined in the damp holds of the ships. Within a year, three-quarters of the women and half the men had died of scurvy or measles. At the First Thanksgiving, in the autumn of 1621, only four women and fifty-three men from the *Mayflower* remained. They bowed to the hospitality of Massasoit (1581–1661), the great sachem of the Algonquian tribe of the Wampanoag of Massachusetts, who would go down in history as the "turkey," the butt of the joke the invaders would play. By 1629 Plymouth had four hundred colonists, and that invasive species had reached about twenty thousand by 1640.

In the following decades, ships from England brought waves of people from debtors' prisons, along with other convicts and adventurers. They would form an odd society ruled by money-hungry, God-fearing Puritans. In the first years of its existence, the New England colony survived on the fur trade, which required an alliance with the local tribes. Competition from the Dutch and a war against the Pequot, who had been decimated by smallpox, characterized that first colonial settlement. A generation after the arrival of the *Mayflower*, relations between the colonists and the indigenous peoples had turned bitter. The war waged by King Philip (1675–78) has gone down in history as the worst tragedy suffered by New England in the seventeenth century. The Algonquian leader Metacomet, whom the English nicknamed "King Philip," was Massasoit's son. That fiery young chief had sworn to push the colonists back into the sea. Twelve English villages were burned, and losses were great on both sides: it is estimated that three thousand Indians were killed and a thousand captives deported to the Bermuda slave market.

It is at this point that the names of the first two Amerindian warrior women make their appearance in the historical record. Weetamoo (c. 1635–1676), sister-in-law to Metacomet, defended the sachem of the Wampanoag, weapons in hand. That unassailable leader, who married five times, led her people against the enemy but drowned in 1676. Her life story defies the stereotype of the submissive Amerindian wife. Awashonks was also a sachem, from the Sakonnet tribe of Rhode Island, and supported Metacomet in his war against the English, then signed a peace treaty with the colonists. In *Women in King Philip's War* (2012), Edward Lodi studies the leadership qualities of these women as fighters and negotiators. In his chapter "Harpies, Housewives, and Heroines," he writes of the cruelties inflicted on the Amerindians by pioneer women, as well as the acts of courage on both sides. The war was hard on colonial women, but it was equally hard on the Amerindian women. Those who survived had the choice between starving to death during

Greeting card with an effigy of the symbolic turkey, 1910.

Weetamoo relentlessly led her people against the enemy. Legend says she died in a river while trying to escape the massacre of her people. From a nineteenth-century engraving.

their escape or being sold as slaves. The English captured King Philip: he was beheaded and his head publicly displayed in Plymouth for twenty years.

At the end of that war, a new sense of colonial American identity was developing. Over the course of the seventeenth century, the cultivation of farmlands, the fur trade, and shipbuilding would usher in an economic boom in New England, the cornerstone of the future American Republic. In about 1641 John Eliot (c. 1604–1690), a Presbyterian clergyman from Massachusetts, translated the Bible into Mohican and Algonquian. His efforts were obliterated by the constant fighting between the colonists and the tribes: in Eliot's own lifetime, the last of the Mohicans who might have read his Bible had vanished. Puritan mercantilism relied on the Holy Book. The parable of Cain and Abel, of the never-ending battle between the hunter and the farmer, had always justified the dispossession of the territories of the indigenous peoples, who lived as nomads on the land and produced nothing. "Where there is a vacant place, there is liberty for the sons of Adam or Noah to come and inhabit." It was God himself who commanded that North America be populated and subjugated. For the Puritans, the very existence of the Indian was an anomaly: without God, without law, without even knee breeches, as Montaigne was amused to remark. They had introduced chaos into the order of things written in the Bible.

American exoticism: here, a young woman from the
Flathead tribe. Painting by Alfred Jacob Miller, 1858.

The Pilgrim Fathers had definite views on women, sin, and fornication: the sad fate awaiting the witches of Salem sums them up. In her *Colonial Intimacies: Indian Marriage in Early New England* (2002), Ann Marie Plane reconstructs the neglected history of the relations between the colonial power and indigenous women through an analysis of travel journals, letters from missionaries, and official archives. They paint an intimate, sometimes tragic picture of the first century and a half of contact. In Virginia, the first law to punish European men and women for having relations with other races dates to 1662. The enlightened interlude of Pocahontas's marriage to John Rolfe had come to an end. Maryland officially banned interracial marriages in 1664, followed by Virginia, which applied the ban to persons of mixed race in 1691. A European woman who gave birth to a mixed-blood child would be condemned with her child to hard labor. This was the beginning of the "blood quantum" or "Indian blood" laws, the aim of which would be to classify populations so as to favor some and discriminate against others. The U.S. Supreme Court did not rule antimiscegenation laws unconstitutional until 1967. Even the term "miscegenation" expresses the old obsession on the part of WASPs with racial mixing. In that view, any intermixing with a nonwhite race would be the cause of genetic decline. The notion of hypodescent emerged at that time—the repellent idea that anyone with a single drop of blood flowing in his or her veins from an ancestor of another race belongs to that race (the one-drop rule). Such a worldview guaranteed that the children of slave women would also be

In nineteenth-century Europe, Amerindians were still a curiosity, as in this portrayal of Iowa individuals visiting London and Paris. Painting by George Catlin, 1861.

slaves. In a sad twist, the same legalistic genealogy is applied in Amerindian tribes today, which require a certain degree of kinship for those seeking to be enrolled as members of the tribe, relying, moreover, on DNA analysis. Cosmopolitan North America has apparently not seen the last of such identity politics.

EIGHTEENTH CENTURY: HISTORIC AMERINDIAN WOMEN IN THE THIRTEEN COLONIES

Racial segregation, then, began to take shape in the thirteen colonies. But as always, prohibition gave rise to transgression. Another love affair, less well known than that of Pocahontas was the relationship between the Iroquois Molly Brant (1736–1796) and Sir William Johnson (1715–1774), superintendent of Indian Affairs for the northern district on behalf of England. Together they had eight children. Molly (or Mary) Brant, born into a Christianized Mohawk family originally from the Province of New York, was the sister of Joseph Brant (1743–1807), an important Iroquois chief allied with the English during the Revolutionary War (1775–

83). She lived in a common-law union with the rich British aristocrat and merchant until his death in 1774. During Sir Johnson's tenure, a period of relatively peaceful coexistence between Anglo-Americans and indigenous peoples reigned. Having been adopted by the Mohawk and having married an Iroquois woman, according to custom Sir Johnson was a heeded adviser, whose position allowed him to recruit Iroquois warriors and lead them into battle and authorized him to sign two treaties in their name. He abused that authority, taking Iroquois land without their realizing it, while at the same time offering them blandishments. During the Seven Years' War against the French (1756–63), Sir Johnson commanded the Iroquois and colonial militias that seized Fort Niagara in 1759, which earned him a certain renown. For the remaining twenty years of his life, he used these militias to maintain the alliance between Iroquois and British interests.

A Seminole of Florida, one of the first portraits of a New World woman. Watercolor by John White, 1585.

Between 1830 and his death in 1872, George Catlin executed hundreds of portraits of Amerindian women across the continent. He said he was documenting a vanishing race. Here Tis-se-wóo-na-tis (She Who Bathes Her Knees), a chief's wife, 1832.

After Johnson died, Brant oversaw her children's education and the family holdings, in keeping with the customs of Iroquois matrilineal society, which give great political weight to women. The authority of the widow was acknowledged among the Iroquois and among the Anglo-Americans. During the Revolutionary War, she joined the Loyalist side and contributed to the British war effort against the Patriots. She eventually took refuge in Kingston, Canada, and died soon after. In 1994 Brant was honored as a Person of National Historical Significance in Canada and was recognized as a true Iroquois and Loyalist heroine. In the United States, she tends to be criticized for taking pro-British positions at the expense of the Iroquois. Is there one truth south of the Great Lakes and another to the north? It appears that Amerindian women often had a role to play in political alliances and divisions.

Mary Musgrove (1700–1767), born Coosaponakeesa, the daughter of a Creek mother and a South Carolina trapper father, was another important historical figure. In about 1730 she married John Musgrove (1695–1735), the first English trader established on the banks of the Savannah River. She served as an intermediary between the Creek and the English colonists seeking to put down roots in Georgia. After the death of her husband in 1735, she continued to exercise her talents as a translator and mediator. Her role as an adviser was recognized by all.

Eighteenth-century U.S. history has also recorded the name of Nancy Ward, or Nanyehi (1738–1822), the last "Beloved Woman" (Ghee Ga Oo) of the Cherokee Nation, heeded adviser and member of the decision-making council of that quasi-gynocratic people. While still young, she participated in attacks against U.S. troops and the invading settlers. On an expedition against the Creek, Ward picked up the rifle of her husband, who had been killed in battle, and led her warriors to victory. The story also goes that Ward saved a captive settler woman about to be burned alive by kicking away the hot embers. "No woman shall be put to death so long as I am Beloved Woman!" she reportedly proclaimed to her people. Until the end of her life, the Beloved Woman of the Cherokee urged them not to give up their land.

THE BLACK INDIANS

Roger Bastide (1898–1974), the anthropologist devoted to the study of African America, was the first in France to analyze the role of sexual attraction and of master/slave couples in the societies of the New World and illuminated the many breaches of the supposed taboo on racial mixing. One statistic he cites is particularly telling: between 1850 and 1860, the mixed-blood population in the United States increased by 67 percent, while the population of slaves increased by only 20 percent. Nevertheless, racial mixing is the skeleton in the closet of U.S. history. Many mixed-race children did not know their father, even if they grew up with their Amerindian or African-American mother. Identifying orphans and legitimizing bastard children would become an obsession in the societies emerging from conquest and slavery. Settlers feared the possibility of alliances between the two oppressed peoples and the demographic consequences.

Slaves fleeing the plantation found refuge in an Amerindian world without fences. *On to Liberty,* a painting by Theodor Kaufmann, 1867.

The military was another path to emancipation. Portrait of a black sergeant and his wife. Photograph of the Pollock studio, c. 1880.

Massacre of the Whites by the Indians and Blacks in Florida.

The above is intended to represent the horrid Massacre of the Whites in Florida, in December 1835, and January, February, March and April 1836, when near Four Hundred (including women and children) fell victims to the barbarity of the Negroes and Indians.

Engraving illustrating the alliance between the fugitive *Nèg'marrons* and the tribes of Florida, formed to massacre the Europeans, 1836.

Black Indians, a category of the population long passed over in silence, were the offspring of slaves who had escaped the plantations (*Nèg'marrons* in the French West Indies) and of Amerindian men and women, primarily in the South. It is said that these were complex relationships: some Amerindian tribes adopted the fugitives, while others used them as slaves. It seems, however, that both parties turned their cultural differences to their advantage. The first black Indians on record date to 1526: fugitive slaves from a Spanish colony in South Carolina took refuge among the indigenous people and set down roots. The Spanish used an unflattering term to designate the black Indian: *Zambo,* which comes from *Zambaigo,* meaning "bowlegged." In 1622 slaves were captured by Amerindians attacking the Jamestown colonists. Gradually integrated into the tribes, these resolute enemies of the English became a worry for the colony. In 1726 the British governor of New York compelled the chiefs of the Iroquois Confederacy to promise to hand over to him any slaves who sought refuge among them. The Europeans attempted to turn the two races into enemies. In 1738 William Henry Lyttelton (1724–1808), governor of South Carolina, wrote: "It has always been the *policy of this government* to create an *aversion* in them [*Indians*] to *Negroes.*" One nation, the Yamassee in Georgia, consisting for the most part of fugitive slaves, long made life difficult for the British troops. In fact, their superior war skills continued to be employed in the Seminole Wars in Florida (beginning in 1817 and continuing sporadically until 1858), in which the tribe and adopted free Africans mounted a united resistance against slavery and racism. Black Seminoles became important leaders. Historians estimate that in about 1820 some eight hundred Africans were living free among the Seminole of Florida. George Catlin, painter of Native Americans, who crisscrossed America like no one else, wrote: "Negro and North American Indian[s], mixed, of equal blood [are . . .] the finest built and most powerful men I have ever yet seen."

In 1866 the U.S. Army formed an African-American cavalry, the famous Buffalo Soldiers celebrated in song by Bob Marley. These soldiers, Seminole scouts among them, would be pitted against Western tribes in the Indian Wars until the 1890s. They would continue to fight in all wars waged by the United States, from the Spanish-American War (1898) to the Philippine-American War (1899–1902) to the expedition to Mexico and Cuba (1916). John Ford's western *Sergeant Rutledge* (1960), which tells the story of an African-American soldier falsely accused of rape and murder, masterfully conveys the atmosphere—a combination of oppressive racism and emancipation through courage and honor—that still surrounds the saga of the Buffalo Soldiers. The last regiment composed exclusively of African-American soldiers was dissolved in 1951, during the Korean War, its soldiers integrated into other units.

Poster for John Ford's film *Sergeant Rutledge,* 1960.

THE GREAT TRIBE
OF THE MÉTIS

The United States, land of freedom and opportunity, is also one of the few countries where the government asks you for your ethnicity. The notorious term "Caucasian" is used only there. Despite such a fastidious categorization of human beings, there is no legal definition of "mixed race." Although Native Americans are recognized, the federal government makes no distinction between those of mixed blood and the others. There could be major consequences were it to do so.

In Canada, a "Métis" is currently defined as a person with mixed aboriginal American and non-aboriginal ancestors. The Canadian Constitution Act of 1982 includes the Amerindians, the Inuit, and the Métis in the laws and treaties that bind the government and the aboriginal peoples of Canada. The Métis National Council was founded in 1983, following that acknowledgment. The major difference between the history of the Canadian Métis and those of mixed race in the United States is that Canadian Métis were not forced to choose between their backgrounds in identifying themselves. In Canada, the law obliges aboriginal people, including Métis, to officially prove their ancestral tribal affiliation. In the absence of scientific data in that field, it is impossible to estimate the quantity of Amerindian blood flowing in the veins of the North American population, any more than one can determine the quantity of the conquerors' blood now mixed with the blood of the surviving aboriginal peoples. Everything suggests that the intermixing was more extensive than official history admits. In 2006, 400,000 people were identified as Métis in Canada. The majority are not the direct offspring of Amerindians and Europeans but the children of Métis, married to other Métis. Over time, the logic of exogamy asserts itself. Geneticists estimate that half the population of western Canada has some Amerindian blood.

The word "Métis" (from the Spanish *mestizo*) originally designated a particular mixed-blood community: the Ottawa or Cree who intermingled with the Scots or French, and more particularly, speakers of the Michif language along the Red

Left: Tsawataineuk girl, from a Pacific Northwest tribe. Photograph by Edward S. Curtis, 1914.

Opposite: Faces of assimilation: portraits of Amerindians and Métis in European dress, between 1868 and 1924.

River, between present-day Manitoba, North Dakota, and Minnesota. Over time, Métis came to designate all the descendants born between the seventeenth and the early nineteenth century to Algonquian women and French and English trappers and traders. Between 1795 and 1815 entire Métis colonies were established in the United States, from Michigan to Wisconsin and from Illinois to Indiana. The economy of the trading posts in these regions was in the hands of the Métis on the frontier. In burgeoning cities, from Chicago to Saint Louis and from Detroit to Prairie du Chien, Wisconsin, Amerindian women, European men, and their Métis children combined their different traditions, inventing a creole language and original values, music, and cuisines. At the same time, these majority-Catholic Métis communities of the Northwest maintained friendship ties and trade relations with the Amerindian tribes.

After the War of 1812, English pioneers began to immigrate en masse from the East Coast to Illinois. By the 1830s, the Métis who spoke French or various creole languages had become the minority in these regions. The fur trade declined, and tribes were relocated west of the Mississippi. Since then, the Métis have adapted in various ways. Those who did not feel welcome in the new capitalist Chicago joined their original tribe in Minnesota or the large Red River Métis colony on the border of Canada. Others settled in the city, married, and integrated into the new society. Even now, however, the Métis of the American Northwest identify as such. They want to make that identity known and seek to develop their heritage between two cultures. As evidence, consider this eloquent proclamation from the United States Métis Nation Inc., concerning the designation "Métis American": "We are the United States Métis Nation. Our ancestors were the original inhabitants of this great land. We also have ancestors that came from across the ocean. We have Native American blood flowing through our veins, yet the tribes of our heritage do not accept us because of this mixture. We are have

Portraits for the National Anthropological Archives: Ida H. Waster, a melancholy "mixed-blood" Kiowa, stares out at us (1896); Mrs. William Whistler, a Fox Métis from the Great Lakes region, poses in a hat (1888).

[*sic*] descended from many great peoples. Having been disenfranchised and marginalized by both ancestral cultures, we now unite to claim our Aboriginal rights. We are a 'Non-Federally Recognized' Indian tribe incorporated as a 'not-for-profit' organization to preserve our culture, our rights, and provide services to our members." The Métis Nation of Indiana adds: "It should also be noted the 'Métis' are not half, as in the term 'half-breed,' of anything. The Métis are not 'part' Native American or 'part' White, or part of any other race for that matter. When the two races were mixed those many years ago an entirely new race was created i.e. 'Métis.' We are not 'part' anything; we are not 'mixed.' An entire new nation, an entire new race of people were born. A new Culture was born: a new language was created; new religion; new mu-

Something new in the West. Métis couple, c. 1910.

sic, dance, and a new way of living was created. The Métis people banded together and they became 'one.' Today it is both correct and proper to consider one's self as 'Full Blooded Métis,' not 'part' anything."

In the northeastern United States as well, the Métis of Maine and the Métis Eastern Tribal Indian Society seek to transmit their culture, particularly by offering initiations into the rite of the medicine wheel of the Eastern Woodland tribes, which teaches harmony and mutual respect for the diverse cultures. In the United States, many organizations of Métis agitate for recognition as an original people with the same rights as the other indigenous peoples. Several million persons of mixed race could lay claim to that heritage, and several thousand have already done so. We know that, over the last three centuries, the Greenlandic Inuit and the Danish colonists intermarried down to the last individual, so that there are no longer any "pure" Greenlanders. According to Alpheus Spring Packard (1839–1905), in Canada the last indigenous "Eskimo," the wife of an English salmon fisher, died in 1859 on the Strait of Belle Isle in Labrador. The union between Newfoundland fisherman fathers and Inuit mothers also produced a large number of descendants in these regions.

For a long time, those of mixed race fascinated and repulsed mainstream culture to an equal degree. Suddenly, from one generation to the next racial mixing has become a good thing, multiracial people are beautiful, café au lait complexions are appreciated, Eurasians are adulated. No doubt we are witnessing a pendulum swing in the other direction, after an obsession with race purity lasting many centuries.

5

First Encounters with the French

THOSE DAMNED ACRES OF SNOW

If Voltaire had only known, those "damned acres" of Canadian snow would have seemed less sterile to him, he who wrote to the kings of France and England that they should stop fighting over so little. During the Enlightenment, those territories of North America had an atmosphere of freedom.

In New France, still only vaguely defined, *coureurs des bois*, fur trappers and traders from France, often turned to the women of the region. Marriages with Amerindian women assured them solid commercial relations with the original occupants, and with their help, the men learned to survive in the new environment. Their freedom was enviable, and their adaptation to the North American wilderness admirable. They wintered with the tribes, learned their languages, participated on the councils, and sometimes fought alongside their indigenous companions. Some trappers told their life stories, recounting the tension of the first contacts and the moments of friendship and intimacy between such different peoples who managed to do business all the same.

For two hundred years, fur was the most important resource in the Province of Quebec, formerly New France. That trade opened up the vast expanses of woods and the western Great Lakes regions to adventurers of all stripes, who satisfied the great European demand for fur, especially beaver pelts, which were highly prized by the hat industry, since they were used in the production of felt. After cod fishing, the beaver felt hat played a determining role in Canada's origins.

Above: Colorized postcard depicting the disembarkment of Jean Nicolet in Green Bay, Wisconsin, 1634.

Opposite: Woman of the West: a Yakama from Washington state, 1899.

The Trapper's Bride,
watercolor by Alfred Jacob
Miller, 1858.

GROW AND PROSPER

Until 1800, when the fur trade was in full swing, many French Canadian trappers intermarried with Wyandot, Cree, Ojibwe, Ottawa, Saulteaux, Assiniboine, Nez Perce, and Gros Ventre. Their Métis children inherited a smattering of Catholicism as well as elements from their indigenous culture, thus becoming a new entity within the North American population. Amerindian wives formed the link between the two worlds. They were valuable partners who prepared furs, sewed clothing, and gathered beneficial plants. As translators, they were able to resolve the cultural antagonisms that might arise. These women proved indispensable for the survival of the adventure seekers in New France. According to the Canadian historian John E. Foster, the process of racial mixing unfolded over two generations. In the first, the employees of the fur companies lived with the tribes and took wives. They later came to settle with their families in the vicinity of trading posts, thereby becoming "House Indians," as the fur companies referred to them. Their children were then often hired by the company. Ultimately, that younger generation would emancipate itself: many of the men became independent trappers, developing a particular culture and language and giving rise to a third generation, the first true Métis.

Their role was central in the conquest of the West. Canada is the "water tower" of the continent, its land blessed with the largest network of rivers and lakes in the world. These provided routes of entry for the birch bark canoes of the *coureurs des bois*, crafts that could cover great distances in a short amount of time, up to forty-five miles a day. In the seventeenth century, Amerindians were still the heart and soul of the fur trade. It was they who hunted beaver, otter, and moose and cleaned the hides. They also wore the furs for a short time after making them; this made the fur even more valuable because it became stronger and silkier. Without that collaboration, the French traders would have had a difficult time making a profit. Over time, the Métis learned to imitate the indigenous peoples' means of survival.

But though Amerindians still made up a large population in New France, their mode of life was threatened. In the first place, many died of diseases brought in by the Europeans. At the same time, the intensity of the fur trade radically changed the traditional relationship between predators and their prey. Amerindian hunters, breaking the age-old totemic contract that bound them to the game they killed, were thrust into the system of commercial profitability imposed by the Europeans. Many abandoned their animist religion and adopted Catholicism. Politics and the church would make good bedfellows.

Left: New France missionary preaching to the Amerindians. Nineteenth-century engraving.

Above: Coureurs des bois bartering with Amerindians. From a drawing by Louis Charles Bombled, 1904.

Return of a French soldier and his Amerindian bride to Fort Orleans,
Missouri, from Paris in 1725. Mural painting in the Missouri state capitol.

This advice given to missionaries provides an indication of the mind-set of
the church: "Win the love of the savages first. Try to bind them to you with little
services, by taking them a burning mirror, for example, to make fire for them during the day, so that they can smoke tobacco. Try hard to eat their sagamité [grits]
without disgust and to take a light meal in the morning, since the barbarians eat
only at sunrise and sunset when they are traveling. Be quick to take your place in
the boat, to disembark nimbly, having taken the precaution to roll up your trousers and shirtsleeves so as not to get them wet. Above all, do not make yourselves
unwelcome with the savages, endure their imperfections without saying a word. If
you must reprimand them, do so with words and signs of love and not with loath-
ing. Do not forget that little presents give the Indians pleasure, supply yourselves
with a half-gross of awls, two or three dozen little knives . . . so as to be able to purchase your food. During porterage, try to assist them, transport a few little things
as your strength allows. Absent pretty words, present a kind face to the Indians
you run into. Do so for Jesus Christ, who is the true source of our greatness, it is he
alone and his cross that we must seek in pursuing those peoples."

THE CALUMET AND
THE FLEUR-DE-LIS

In 1625 the first contingent of Jesuits landed in Quebec and established the mission
of Sainte-Marie-among-the-Hurons. In 1627 Cardinal Richelieu created the Company of One Hundred Associates, to which he entrusted control of the fur trade.
In 1642, on an island in the Saint Lawrence River more than nine hundred miles
inland, the Sulpicians Jean-Jacques Olier de Verneuil (1608–1657) and Jérôme

Le Royer (1597–1659) founded the Society of Our Lady of Montreal to convert the indigenous peoples of New France. The bartering of animal hides for other goods intensified, and Montreal became the meeting place for the Wyandot and French traders.

But *la belle province* in the process of formation had a difficult time recruiting settlers. In 1680 there were 493 inhabitants, whereas, that same year, Intendant Duschesneau (d. 1696) estimated the number of French living in the woods at eight hundred. Colbert, Louis XIV's minister of finance, discovered that a large number of young men were leaving the colony and vanishing for years to trade in remote regions. Their primary motivations were the lure of profit ensured by the fur trade and the almost total absence of women in the colonies. To keep the colony from becoming depopulated, Colbert organized a system of *congés de traite* (trade leaves), which allowed only twenty-five *coureurs des bois* three canoe expeditions a year to engage in commerce in the West.

Colbert would not succeed in halting the drain. By the eighteenth century, mixed marriages would find favor with the missionaries as well. In Missouri and Illinois, most families of French descent have Amerindian blood. The establishment of trading posts such as Detroit fostered fruitful unions.

Throughout that period, the French traders were in bitter competition with the Hudson's Bay Company, and the French took the lion's share. They enjoyed several advantages: they controlled the principal waterways throughout the frontier; they had at their disposal all the birch bark necessary to produce canoes (which the English were completely without); and they had formed strong kin-ship ties with the indigenous peoples. By contrast, the Hudson's Bay Company discouraged unions between traders and Amerindians. Furthermore, the English of the thirteen colonies were attempting to obtain more territories for colonization, and that annoyed the tribes they were infringing on. (The French did not covet the new territory, but they were determined to deprive the English of it.) All the same, there were Anglo-Métis children of the fur trade: communities of what were called "Countryborn" developed original creole languages such as Bungee, a mix of Gaelic and Algonquian still spoken in those northern latitudes.

Portrait of Wa-quóth-e-qua. Painting by George Catlin, 1835.

COUREURS DES BOIS AND "WHITE INDIANS"

A few names of famous *coureurs des bois* have come down to us. Their experiences inspired a number of U.S. writers, from James Fenimore Cooper to Jack London, and thrilled generations of teenagers. It was these trappers who best personified the sense of freedom that could be experienced by tramping through a new world. They embody the allure of the Amerindian life in mainstream culture because by their assimilation they bridge the two by essentially becoming "white Indians." Étienne Brûlé (1592–1633), having arrived in Canada at the age of sixteen, was the first European to venture into the Erie, Ontario, and Michigan Great Lakes region to engage in the fur trade. In 1615 Brûlé served as a go-between/interpreter for the explorations of Samuel de Champlain (c. 1567–1635). What is remembered of Brûlé's colorful life is that he was the first to become a Wyandot, the first to embrace their customs and intermarry, and alas, the first to be killed and consumed by those same Wyandot. In Montreal, a park and a school are named after him.

Louis Jolliet (1645–1700) was also responsible for important explorations. Sent by Governor Frontenac (1622–1698) on a mission of observation and negotiation among the tribes living along the Mississippi, he navigated that great river in 1673–74, venturing six hundred miles from its mouth. Pierre-Esprit Radisson (1636–1710) was another interesting figure from that era, as attested by the titles of the biographies devoted to him: *Merchant, Adventurer, White Indian and Double Agent, Coureur des Bois and Man of the World*. That Parisian, who would die in London, arrived in New France in 1652. Captured during an Iroquois raid and adopted by the tribe, Radisson became a *coureur des bois*, shifting back and forth between French and English traders. He was renowned for the cargoes of furs he brought to Trois-Rivières in more than a hundred canoes. A city in northern Quebec and a metro station in Montreal bear his name.

Médard Chouart des Groseilliers (1618–1696) arrived in New France at the age of sixteen and joined a mission of Jesuit fathers among the Wyandot. He would remain with them for ten years and become a *coureur des bois*. In the company of his friend Radisson, he explored

Opposite: Oregon Madonna, c. 1905.

Above: The *coureur des bois* Étienne Brûlé camps at the mouth of the Humber River. Painting by Frederick Sproston Challener, 1956.

northern Ontario and was the first European to reach Lake Superior. He died in Trois-Rivières in 1696. Jean Nicolet (1598–1642), a clerk for the Compagnie des Marchands de Rouen et de Saint-Malo, was nineteen when he arrived in New France in 1618. For two years he lived among the Algonquian and the Wyandot on the Ottawa River, along the fur route. Nicolet became the interpreter and recognized intermediary between the settlers and the tribes. In about 1630 he married an Amerindian woman. The Nicolets would become one of the most important Métis families in the region. At the request of the king of France and Champlain, Nicolet went off to explore the western lands, searching for a hypothetical Chinese Sea. He was the first European to reach Lake Huron and Wisconsin. Legend has it that he had brought back from a visit to China a silk tunic embroidered with multicolored flowers and birds, which he put on in front of the Ho-Chunk, thinking he had reached the road to Cathay. That is said to have made a great impression on the indigenous peoples. Chequamegon-Nicolet National Forest and the city of Nicolet, Wisconsin, are named for him.

Other succinct biographies mention long-ago encounters. In about 1720 Jean-Baptiste Rémaune (b. 1675), former interpreter to the king of France at Fort Saint Joseph but an illegal trafficker all the same, married Simphorose Ouaougoukoue (1700–1747), an Illinois woman who assured him many descendants, the good graces of her people, and made his fortune. Likewise, the marriage of the fur trader Michel Accault to Aramepinchiewe, daughter of the Illinois chief, fostered the trade in skins but also the establishment of the Jesuit Mission of the Immaculate Conception of Our Lady in the Great Lakes region. Aramepinchiewe, a

Landing of Jean Nicolet at Lake Michigan in Wisconsin in 1634.
He would be the first European to reach that region. Illustration
inspired by a painting by Edwin Willard Deming, 1904.

The network of Canada's waterways opened the country to the explorers
Radisson and Chouart des Groseilliers. Painting by Frederic Remington, 1905.

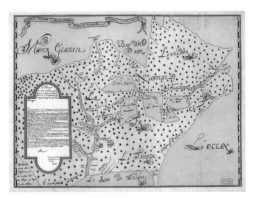

Map from *Relations des jésuites*
in 1673 showing the location of
several nations in New France.

Samuel de Champlain's defeat of the Iroquois,
opening the way for the colonization of New
France in the early 1600s. After an engraving,
Les voyages du Sieur de Champlain, 1613.

Trapper and his Amerindian wife, painting by Alfred Jacob Miller, 1837.

convert to Christianity, brought a number of her people to the church as Father Superior Jacques Gravier (1651–1708) liked to mention in his letters. So it went for New France, land of missions and of commercial and conjugal ties.

By the end of the seventeenth century, the French had made the Missouri River a potential access route from Louisiana to the mythical "Western Sea," that is, the Pacific. Étienne Véniard, sieur de Bourgmont (1679–1734), who visited the Missouri people in 1714, established a short-lived alliance between the river tribes—Missouri, Otoe, Osage, Kansas, Pawnee, Iowa, and others—and the Plains Apache in 1723–24; he also built Fort Orleans (abandoned in 1728). In 1738 Pierre Gaultier de Varennes, sieur de La Vérendrye (1685–1749), reached the "land of the Mandans," in his case from Canada, and in 1742 two of his sons went as far as the Black Hills of South Dakota. But though a handful of *coureurs des bois* chose to settle among the indigenous peoples, the French colonial authorities did not create the imperial infrastructure—trading posts, missions, garrisons—in those remote regions that had made for the success of their alliances with the peoples of the Great Lakes region and the Mississippi Valley. Saint Louis was founded in 1764 by the French, who began to visit Missouri on a regular basis. By 1800 French fur merchants of Canadian origin (called Canadiens) and Louisianans (Creoles) were pushing ever deeper into the West.

Jean-Baptiste Pointe du Sable (1745–1818), another important individual of mixed race, has been largely forgotten by history. Born in Saint-Domingue in 1745 to an African slave mother and a French sailor father, he received his education in France, then headed for Louisiana. Having traveled up the Mississippi, he founded a trading post along the Chicago River, the resupply point for *coureurs des bois*, traders, and Amerindians, who called the place "Chicagoua" ("wild onion"). In 1778, in the Catholic church of Cahokia, Illinois, Pointe du Sable married Kittihawa (Catherine), daughter of a Potawatomi chief. They had two children, Jean and Suzanne, the first to be officially recorded in Chicago. During the Revolutionary War, Pointe du Sable fought alongside the French and the American colonists. With the help of the Amerindians, he mounted a resistance to the British. After the United States had won its independence, he became an explorer and pioneer, the first owner of a residence in Chicago, as well as a distiller and entrepreneur. He made several trips to Canada. After him, many Métis families from New France arrived to establish the fur trade in Chicago. Pointe du Sable died in Saint Charles, Missouri, on August 28, 1818.

Voltaire, of course, did not celebrate the epic of New France in North America, seeing only war, commerce, and religious proselytism. The philosopher might also have seen—and this would have been more original—the signs of deep relationships between two worlds, which would produce a third.

Left: Sioux girl, painting by Alfred Jacob Miller, 1860.

Above: Postage stamp in honor of Jean-Baptiste Pointe du Sable, founding father of Chicago, 1987.

6

A Young Nation in the Nineteenth Century

YOUTHFUL PASSIONS

Ideas changed rapidly after the American Revolution. Thomas Jefferson, the third president of the United States, had humanistic views on the cosmopolitanism that was his country's destiny. During his tenure, he asked citizens to go out and get to know the indigenous peoples, to mingle with them, to become one nation. And he practiced the integrated view he preached: in 1998 DNA analyses proved that Jefferson had fathered several children with his half-African slave Sally Hemings (c. 1773–1835), whom he would eventually emancipate.

During the same period, patriot Patrick Henry (1736–1799) proposed that marriages between Europeans and Amerindians should be encouraged through tax subsidies and cash payments. That new frame of mind found form in the colorful life story of Samuel Houston (1793–1863), for which the Texas city is named. The son of a general, Houston ran off to the Tennessee mountains to live with the Cherokee while he was still an adolescent, then joined the war against the English. He was wounded three times. He went on to study law, became a lawyer, and tried his hand at politics. Houston was elected governor of Tennessee in 1827 but resigned in 1829, returning to live among his Cherokee friends. He was adopted by them and married a mixed-race woman, with whom he ran a trading post. In about 1830 Houston showed up in Washington, DC, dressed as a Cherokee, to denounce the fraud committed by government agents against the Cherokee Nation. He had to flee the capital after a duel with William Stanbery (1788–1873), U.S.

Above: A dream of integration: the offspring of President Jefferson and his slave Sally Hemings. Nineteenth-century engraving.

Opposite: Portrait of a young Arikara from Nebraska. Photograph by Edward S. Curtis, 1908.

representative from Ohio. In 1835 when Texas seceded from Mexico, Houston was given command of the Texian army to wage the war of independence. On October 22, 1836, Houston became the first (and only) president of the new Republic of Texas, a nation larger than France but short-lived, given its ineluctable incorporation, in 1845, into U.S. territory.

Despite the social upheavals arising from the American Revolution, interracial unions were still poorly regarded. The official legislation of the new federal government would long perpetuate the segregationist laws of the British colonies in the United States. Nevertheless, at the dawn of the nineteenth century, a young Shoshone woman would be called on to personify, more than any other, the history of the young nation's conquest of the West.

Photograph of the unthinkable,
a woman of European descent
with an Amerindian, c. 1900.

SACAGAWEA AND THE LEWIS AND CLARK EXPEDITION

U.S. hagiography has mythicized two Amerindian woman: Pocahontas, the open-armed Powhatan of Virginia, and Sacagawea (1788–1812), the young Shoshone on the Lewis and Clark expedition (1804–06). Her real likeness will remain forever unknown, but she had the signal honor of appearing with her child on the U.S. golden dollar coin. Sacagawea is also one of two Amerindian women whose bronze portraits stand in the National Statuary Hall of the U.S. Capitol in Washington, DC, along with ninety-eight other national heroes. There she is honored as a "traveler and guide, a translator, a diplomat, and a wife and mother," in recognition of "her indomitable spirit," "a decided factor in the success of Lewis and Clark's . . . expedition." That undertaking was of major importance: the explorers set out to open the "gateway to the West" for the impetuous American Republic, which sought to extend its influence beyond the East Coast while thwarting the European powers still present on the continent: the English in the north,

First dollar struck with the effigy of
an Amerindian woman: Sacagawea
and her papoose, 2000.

Reproduction of the journal kept by William Clark during the Lewis and Clark expedition.

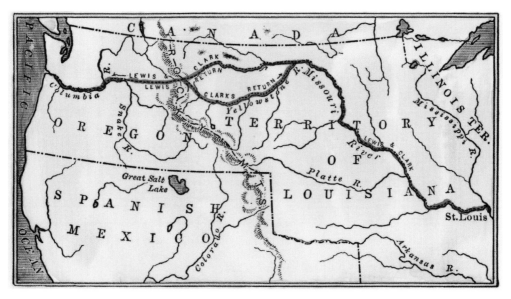

Map of the itinerary of the Corps of Discovery, from Saint Louis to Fort Clatsop.
Nineteenth-century engraving.

Everywind, an Ojibwe. Photograph by Roland W. Reed, 1907.

Curiosities of the New World: the flattening of children's skulls by the Flathead.
Drawing by William Clark, from his journal.

the French in Louisiana Territory, and the Spanish in Florida and the Southwest. With the Louisiana Purchase of 1803 from Napoleon Bonaparte, the United States claimed the entire Midwest but would still have to foil Canadian English designs on the unknown territories of the West. President Jefferson decided to organize an expedition to reach the Pacific Coast, and he persuaded Congress to allocate twenty-five hundred dollars for the project.

Captains Meriwether Lewis (1774–1809) and William Clark (1770–1838) led that scientific and commercial mission: their aim was to draw maps, gain knowledge of the unknown tribes, make botanical discoveries, and do an assessment of the fur-bearing animals. The two left a precise and frank journal of their trip. On May 13, 1804, the Corps of Discovery (forty men in two pirogues and a keelboat) left Saint Louis and traveled up the Missouri. From there, they crossed the Rocky Mountains to the banks of the Pacific, following the Oregon Trail. That terra incognita had no need of bold explorers to acknowledge its existence, despite what Lewis sought to suggest when he wrote: "We were now about to penetrate a country at least two thousand miles in width, on which the foot of civilized

Captain Clark, envoy of Thomas Jefferson, the "Great Father in Washington," meets peoples of the Columbia River Plateau, with whom contact had never before been made. Painting by Charles M. Russell, 1897.

man had never trodden." Among those Lewis would consider civilized there were the French fur traders, who were already journeying from the Great Lakes to the Rockies; the Russians, who often visited the northern Pacific Coast from the other direction; and the Spaniards settled in California.

The Corps of Discovery established contact with some thirty indigenous groups belonging to three cultural zones—the Plains, the Columbia Plateau, and the Pacific Northwest Coast—each with its own history, social and political organization, kinship system, and myths. The expedition could not have achieved its goal without the aid of the indigenous peoples, suppliers of food and horses, guides, and commercial allies.

The success of the expedition was due in part to the presence of the young Shoshone Sacagawea, wife of the Canadian trapper Toussaint Charbonneau (1767–1843), who had won her in a game of chance and married her when she was fifteen. Sacagawea met the expedition at Fort Mandan, the explorers' starting point on their way to the Rocky Mountains. Clark wrote: "A french man by Name Chabonah [Charbonneau], who Speaks the Big Belley language visit us . . . we engau [engaged] him to go on with us and take one of his wives to interpret the Snake [Shoshone] language." Sacagawea's knowledge of the people and environments along the way saved the expedition at least twice: first, when she prevented the

The beginnings of anthropology: *American Nations,* lithograph from the German encyclopedia *Meyers Konversations-Lexikon* (1839–55).

An icon takes shape: Sacagawea guiding Lewis and Clark. Painting by N. C. Wyeth, 1939.

The adventures of the Lewis and Clark expedition. Engraving by A. Sargent, published in *The Illustrated Universe*, 1881.

party from losing food and documents in the rapids; and second, when the expedition came into contact with the Shoshone, which was at first a hostile meeting but whose chief was none other than her brother Cameahwait. The young woman could have remained with him and her people, but she decided to continue the journey. Her feat was all the more commendable in that she gave birth to a son during the expedition and also had to endure her husband's abuse throughout the trip. After Sacagawea's death, Captain Clark took over custody of the child born en route to the Pacific, Jean-Baptiste Charbonneau (1805–1866). He too would have a very adventurous life: first in Europe, where he was able to gain access to the royal courts and salons as a minor celebrity; then in the American West, where he became in succession a gold prospector, an alcade (magistrate), and a Mormon.

Another Amerindian woman helped the Lewis and Clark mission through a rough spell: Wat-ku-ese, who had been uprooted and forced to move several times. In the 1770s the Nez Perce and the Salish had set up camp in a valley of the Bitterroot Mountains. Their camp was attacked by the Blackfoot, and the women and children abducted. A little Nez Perce girl was traded to the Cree in the north, who in turn traded her to a Chippewa group to the east. This was the beginning of a captivity that would last thirty years. The woman was later sold to a settler in Canada, who treated her well. He entrusted her to a Crow group, who returned her to the Salish; from there, she could finally return to the Nez Perce, in about 1804. Her tribe gave her the name "Wat-ku-ese" ("she who was lost and found"). She told them her long story, saying that, far to the east, there was a very powerful people with light skin, hair on their faces, and rimmed crowns (hats) on their heads, and that they had in fact saved her life. She called them *So-yap-po.* Her people thought she had lost her mind, not believing such things could exist. Nevertheless a few months later, the strange creatures she described made their appearance in the members of the Lewis and Clark expedition. Wat-ku-ese's endorsement forestalled any hostile confrontation. The powerful Nez Perce might otherwise have killed or captured the explorers and seized their wealth, but the intervention in their favor by an old woman of the tribe secured them a friendly welcome.

Marie Iowa Dorion (1786–1850) was another woman to cross half of North America. Six years after Sacagawea, this Métis of Iowa descent reached the mouth of the Columbia River under near-impossible conditions: she was pregnant and had her two little children along. She was accompanying her husband Pierre Dorion, who had lived among the Yankton for some twenty years and was hired as an interpreter and guide for the Astor expedition (1810–12). For reasons unknown, this formidable woman's achievements have escaped mythicization.

Progress of natural sciences: William Clark's drawing of a trout, a page from his journal.

A NATION OF TRADERS

In the name of the United States, Lewis and Clark were charged with establishing relations of allegiance with the tribes they encountered, by introducing the metaphor of the "Great Father in Washington." To better control the region, the captains adopted Caesar's methods in the Gaul of the Pax Romana—distributing presents and dividing to conquer—in order to impose the Pax Americana. Shoshone petty chiefs demanded as many gifts as the great chief Cameahwait—a real headache for his sister Sacagawea, who had to speak in the name of the explorers. During their journey, the two captains distributed medals, certificates, military uniforms, flags, hats, and other such items. The corps came to play the role of suppliers. Ever since Christopher Columbus, it had been believed that presents were indispensable for any foray into new territory, and Lewis had stocked up in Saint Louis: glass beads, copper buttons, knives, axes, cooking pots, tobacco, mirrors, scissors, needles, fishhooks. GIs would do the same in 1944, with nylon stockings and chewing gum. The Amerindians themselves brought back from their raids horses and captives—especially women and children, who were either adopted or enslaved. The young Shoshone Sacagawea had in this manner been taken by the Hidatsa.

The young U.S. government would conduct a policy of establishing trading posts and forts, which would turn the indigenous peoples into hounded debtors, dispossessed of their hunting lands and ultimately dumped on reservations. We are indebted to Gilles Havard, a historian of European/Amerindian exchanges, for the following reflections: "In pushing the Indians to bury the hatchet and to bring back furs from their expeditions rather than scalps, the U.S. president intended to build a peaceful commercial empire, while at the same time driving the British off the Plains. . . . But the Indians perceived peace merely as a truce, and from one day to the next could go from commercial trade to warfare. . . . The reaction of the various tribes depended on whether they had previously been integrated into the commercial networks and whether they were acquainted with

Song of the eagle becoming one with the storm. Painting by N. C. Wyeth, 1916.

Ho-Chunk encampment. Painting by Seth Eastman, 1847.

the whites. The Shoshone, the Salish, and the Nez Perce had enjoyed few of the advantages of Euro-American trade before that time and may have had much more to gain than the others from an alliance with Lewis and Clark. The Shoshone, lacking firearms, suffered bitterly from the raids of their Blackfeet and Hidatsa enemies. By contrast, the Chinook and the Clatsop, thanks to their occasional relations with European or American merchants on the Pacific Coast, already possessed rifles, cooking pots, textile products, and so on, and had in fact become shrewd negotiators. . . . Lewis and Clark were generally able to avoid deadly confrontations with the Indians. On the whole, friendly relations prevailed, based on a mutual desire for alliances. Each side sought to assure itself of the good intentions of the other and to establish a climate of trust indispensable for establishing a cordial relationship. Lewis and Clark were the heirs to several decades of Euro-Amerindian diplomacy. The French, who in the seventeenth century had been the first to enter into contact with the autochthonous people in the interior of the continent, were renowned for their capacity to adapt to the protocol of their hosts—rituals of gifts and countergifts, peace pipe ceremony, metaphorical language of kinship, and so on. During the encounter with the Shoshone (August 13, 1805), Lewis readily agreed to subscribe to Amerindian etiquette."

It is easy to imagine the leaders of the Corps of Discovery stopped for the evening, smoking the calumet with their hosts, dreaming of the vast commercial market they were about to open, and anticipating, with the help of the tobacco, a network of forts and trading posts throughout the Far West. Such a vision would have prefigured the U.S. territory as it now exists, studded with giant shopping malls and military bases.

SEXUAL HOSPITALITY IN THE NEW WORLD

As it happens, the sexual hospitality of certain tribes on the North American continent was renowned, and "the rites of Venus" in North America an object of fantasy. It can be inferred that the perception of such relations was very different among the indigenous peoples than it was for their European visitors, who provide most of our historical record on the subject.

Mandan villages served as a commercial rendezvous point for the traders of Canada, who bartered horses and firearms for furs from the Crow, Cheyenne, Assiniboine, Kiowa, and Arapaho of the northern Great Plains. Captain Bossu (1720–1792) wrote in his *Nouveaux voyages en Indes occidentales* (*New Journeys to the West Indies*, 1768): "The polite thing for the savages is to offer us girls. As a result, the chiefs go about haranguing the villagers in the morning, saying: Young men and warriors, don't be crazy; love the Master of life; hunt to feed the French, who bring us what we need; and you, young ladies, do not be difficult or ungrateful toward the white warriors about having some of their blood; it is through that alliance that we will have the same spirit they do and will be feared by our enemies."

Left: Two young Apache. Photograph by Frank A. Rinehart, 1898.

Opposite: A young Tolowa from Oregon in traditional dress; her people did not meet the European settlers until the nineteenth century. Photograph by Edward S. Curtis, 1923.

Above: Portrait of a Navajo woman.
Photograph by Edward S. Curtis, 1904.

Opposite: Hopi woman. Photograph by
Edward S. Curtis, 1905.

Gilles Havard, who explored the question of sexual hospitality toward the Europeans between the seventeenth and nineteenth centuries, has concluded that the practice is somewhat akin to "spiritual hypergamy," by which the Europeans transmitted their power to Amerindian men by having sexual relations with their women. Havard's analysis of the Lewis and Clark journals sheds new light on that encounter between the two worlds: "Everywhere, the intimacy of contact found expression in sexual relations, which linked members of the expedition to particularly enterprising Indian women. Offering one's body was not experienced as a form of prostitution by the autochthonous peoples, who respected certain taboos but were unfamiliar with the Christian notion of sins of the flesh. The sexual act was not problematized from a moral standpoint as it is in the West and, like the exchange of food and objects, constituted a way of making contact with the other. Beyond sex, intermarriage was perceived by the Indians as a means for integrating the traders into the circle of kinship and thus for assuring that the group would be resupplied."

Clark noted that, among the Teton, his refusals were viewed as an insult and fueled tensions between that group and the explorers. Clark's hesitations evaporated among the Arikara, the women of whom his companion Sergeant John Ordway judged "very handsome." Likewise, it was no coincidence that Mandan villages were the traders' rendezvous point. "It may be observed generally that chastity is not very highly esteemed by these people," Sergeant Patrick Gass exclaimed indignantly of the Shoshone women.

But in spite of any scruples they may have had, the men yielded to temptation. As Lewis wrote: "To prevent this mutual exchange of good officies altogether I know it impossible to effect, particularly on the part of our young men whom some months abstanence have made very polite to those tawney damsels." At Fort Clatsop, the women came to offer their favors in exchange for bits of ribbon, fishhooks, or beads. "Those people appear to View Sensuality as a necessary evile," writes Clark. "The young females are fond of the attention of our men." According to Havard in *The Lewis and Clark Expedition*, "these sexual unions had three consequences: they shored up the alliance between the explorers and the autochthonous peoples; they gave rise to a few cases of syphilis; . . . and finally, these affairs contributed to racial mixing."

Benjamin Armstrong, an Englishman who had traded with the Ojibwe in the 1840s, married the chief's daughter. In his *Indians of North America: Social Life and Customs* (1892), he writes that it was impossible to conduct business without marrying a woman of the clan as the only assurance of a long-term contract. In those regions, when a man wanted to marry, he went into the forest and killed an animal. The woman he desired was supposed to accept that meat and prepare it. Only then would the couple's parents grant their permission. In Ojibwe folklore, there is a story of a woman who married a beaver which illustrates the perceived benefits of interracial marriage: the beaver gives its fur and, in exchange, takes home iron goods. Women—as negotiators, emissaries, sexual partners, wives, and members of a large family network—formed the bridge between cultures.

THE TRAIL OF TEARS

After former French president Nicolas Sarkozy's rash "Dakar speech" about nations that have not yet entered history, it is no doubt necessary to reaffirm that all peoples have a history, including the Amerindians, who witnessed an expansion in their populations, adapted to diverse environments, established vast networks of commercial exchanges, and waged internecine and intertribal wars: that was their reality. In spite of this, Europeans had a way of justifying their conquests by elaborating a mythic image of the New World, portrayed as virgin land just waiting to offer itself. To hear them tell it, Christopher Columbus's arrival brought to a definitive end a timeless prehistoric era in which the first inhabitants of the continent had been living. The indeterminate origin of these indigenous peoples also contributed to their mythicization. First the explorers, then the missionaries, and afterward the settlers provided fanciful responses to that enigma. For some, Amerindians were descended from one of the lost tribes of Israel; for others, they came from the lost continent of Atlantis or had reached the Americas in Noah's ark. A later and more perverse myth labeled them "savages" who had been killing one another for centuries and whose last wandering hordes had to be placed on reservations. In 1803, when President Jefferson secured the Louisiana Purchase, he believed that those immense territories, to be shared by

INDIAN LAND FOR SALE

GET A HOME
OF
YOUR OWN

EASY PAYMENTS

PERFECT TITLE

POSSESSION
WITHIN
THIRTY DAYS

FINE LANDS IN THE WEST

| IRRIGATED IRRIGABLE | GRAZING | AGRICULTURAL DRY FARMING |

In 1910 the Department of the Interior Sold Under Sealed Bids Allotted Indian Land as Follows:

Location.	Acres.	Average Price per Acre.	Location.	Acres.	Average Price per Acre.
Colorado	5,211.21	$7.27	Oklahoma	34,664.00	$19.14
Idaho	17,013.00	24.85	Oregon	1,020.00	15.43
Kansas	1,684.50	33.45	South Dakota	120,445.00	16.53
Montana	11,034.00	9.86	Washington	4,879.00	41.37
Nebraska	5,641.00	36.65	Wisconsin	1,069.00	17.00
North Dakota	22,610.70	9.93	Wyoming	865.00	20.64

FOR THE YEAR 1911 IT IS ESTIMATED THAT 350,000 ACRES WILL BE OFFERED FOR SALE

For information as to the character of the land write for booklet, "INDIAN LANDS FOR SALE," to the Superintendent U. S. Indian School at any one of the following places:

WALTER L. FISHER,
Secretary of the Interior.

ROBERT G. VALENTINE,
Commissioner of Indian Affairs.

The West at a bargain price: notice of sale of territories taken from the tribes by the U.S. government, 1887.

The Trail of Tears: the expulsion of all the indigenous peoples from the southeastern states is a dark stain on U.S. history (1831–36). Painting by Robert Lindneux, 1942.

the Amerindians and the settlers, would suffice. Within a generation, however, it became clear to the powers that be that the tribal peoples would have to make room. Between 1806 and 1830, fifty tribes still living as nomads on U.S. territories were relocated. When negotiations did not effect a complete removal, President Andrew Jackson (1767–1845) sent in the troops.

On May 28, 1830, Congress passed the Indian Removal Act, which expelled all Amerindians from the southeastern states and settled them in territories west of the Mississippi. The "Five Civilized Tribes" of the Seminole, Cherokee, Choctaw, Chickasaw, and Creek still living east of the Mississippi, who had already been forced to abandon nomadism and collective property and to take up farming, were nevertheless exiled to reservations in Oklahoma. Between 1831 and 1836, forty-six thousand Choctaw, Chickasaw, and Creek were driven from their homes. Alexis de Tocqueville (1805–1859), who was traveling in the region at the time, witnessed that scene, which, in horror, he describes in *De la démocratie en Amérique* (*Democracy in America*, 1835 and 1840): "At the end of the year 1831, while I was on the left [east] bank of the Mississippi, at a place named by Europeans Memphis, there arrived a numerous band of Choctaws. . . . These . . . had left their country and were endeavoring to gain the right bank of the Mississippi, where they hoped

Opposite: Cheyenne mother and her child. Photograph by L. A. Huffman, c. 1890.

Above: The sacred circle grows smaller: Miniconjou on their reservation in South Dakota, 1890.

Lucy, survivor of the massacres of the western conquest, photographed at the presumed age of 120, for the Washington State Historical Society, 1911.

to find an asylum that had been promised them by the American government. It was then the middle of winter, and the cold was unusually severe; the snow had frozen hard upon the ground, and the river was drifting huge masses of ice. The Indians had their families with them, and they brought in their train the wounded and the sick, with children newly born and old men upon the verge of death. They possessed neither tents nor wagons, but only their arms and some provisions. I saw them embark to pass the mighty river, and never will that solemn spectacle fade from my remembrance. No cry, no sob, was heard among the assembled crowd; all were silent. Their calamities were of ancient date, and they knew them to be irremediable."

The Seminole, in alliance with fugitive slaves, waged war against the invaders for a long time, before being deported by boat to be used as slaves in Bermuda. In 1838 President Martin Van Buren (1782–1862) sent General Winfield Scott (1786–1866) to evacuate the Cherokee from their territory in Georgia at gunpoint. Twenty thousand men, women, and children were thrust onto the Trail of Tears, a forced march of twenty-two hundred miles to Oklahoma. The episode is still a dark stain on U.S. history. Four thousand of them starved, froze to death, or died of exhaustion. A few Cherokee women who survived to tell the story are still

Caroline Elizabeth ("Carrie")
Bushyhead, a Cherokee who
survived the Trail of Tears as
a child, 1903.

A meaningful look: portrait of Nasuteas, a Kichai
woman from Wichita, Kansas. Photograph by Frank
Rinehart, 1898.

remembered, such as Elizabeth Brown Stephens (1821–1846). Quatie Ross (c. 1790–
1839), the wife of Chief John Ross (1790–1866), also recounted the sufferings of the
Cherokee—sick, starving, with only muddy water to drink and thin blankets to
share among them. Two survivors of the Trail of Tears, Watt Christie (1817–1902)
and his wife, Lydia (c. 1828–1875), had a son, Ned Christie (1852–1892), a member
of the Cherokee council, who was shot down by a sheriff in 1892 for a murder he
did not commit. He is now honored by his people as a martyr. Caroline Elizabeth
("Carrie") Bushyhead (1834–1903), born on the Trail of Tears to Baptist Cherokee
parents, was another of the rare survivors able to bear witness to that tragic episode in the conquest of North America.

MANIFEST DESTINY

"[It] is . . . our manifest destiny to overspread and to possess the whole of the continent which Providence has given us for the development of the great experiment of liberty and federated self-government entrusted to us." That ideology of expansion, so defined by the New York journalist John O'Sullivan (1813–1895) in 1845, asserted the messianic character of the irreversible colonization of the North American continent by Anglo-Saxons from the East Coast. Before him, the Pilgrim Fathers had proclaimed their divine right to populate the continent and there to establish their great institutions, superior to the hidebound ones existing in Europe. President James Monroe (1758–1831) reasserted that right in 1823. According to the Monroe Doctrine, the Old World belonged to the Europeans, the New World to the Americans, a view that justified the expansion of the United States into the West. An isolationist vis-à-vis the rest of the world, Monroe was interventionist and hegemonic at home. Throughout the nineteenth century, successive U.S. administrations would set about to increase tenfold their territorial holdings: in 1803, the Louisiana Purchase in and of itself doubled the territory of the United States. In 1846 the Oregon Treaty gave the United States an oceanfront view of the Pacific; in 1848 the outcome of the Mexican-American War earned the nation an

Manifest Destiny of the Americans, on the march to civilize the West.
Painting by John Gast, 1872.

additional 500,000 square miles; then came the purchase of Alaska from Russia in 1867. A hundred years of Indian Wars, ending only in 1890 at Wounded Knee, would deliver up the Far West. Finally, the annexation of Hawaii with the assistance of the U.S. Marines, who deposed the last queen of the archipelago in 1893, ended the expansion, though Arizona would not join the Union until 1912.

The Amerindians, whose views were completely at odds with those of the expanding nation, represented an obstacle. If they were not to vanish, they had to adopt the "American way of life." Reservations were used to marginalize, on uncultivable lands, those who resisted handing over their land to the settlers. The always-perspicacious Tocqueville notes: "The expulsion of the Indians often takes place at the present day in a regular and, as it were, a legal manner." As evidence, he quotes the remarks of John Bell, chair of the Committee on Indian Affairs, who declared to Congress on February 24, 1830: "To pay an Indian tribe what their ancient hunting grounds are worth to them after the game is fled or destroyed, as a mode of appropriating wild lands claimed by Indians, has been found more convenient, and certainly it is more agreeable to the forms of justice, as well as more merciful, than to assert the possession of them by the sword. Thus the practice of buying Indian titles is only the substitute which humanity and expediency have imposed, in place of the sword, in arriving at the actual enjoyment of property claimed by the right of discovery, and sanctioned by the natural superiority allowed to the claims of civilized communities over those of savage tribes."

Tocqueville sagely concluded: "The Spaniards were unable to exterminate the Indian race by those unparalleled atrocities which brand them with indelible shame, nor did they succeed even in wholly depriving it of its rights; but the Americans of the United States have accomplished this twofold purpose with singular felicity, tranquilly, legally, philanthropically, without shedding blood, and without violating a single great principle of morality in the eyes of the world. It is impossible to destroy men with more respect for the laws of humanity."

Encampment of Sioux at the Battle of Wounded Knee, 1890.

The Lakota chief Big Foot lying in bloody snow at Wounded Knee.
Photograph by Clarence G. Morledge, 1890.

Opening day for the sale of land purchased from the Cheyenne in Oklahoma,
organized by the U.S. government, 1893.

Tepees would now house sewing machines. Photograph by T. A. Morris, 1906.

THE RESERVATIONS

Reservations do not project a flattering image of the United States: the short life expectancy of their occupants, the high infant mortality rate, and the problems of malnutrition, alcoholism, and drug use almost make them subsistence-level enclaves within the richest nation in the world. The Pine Ridge Reservation in South Dakota is often cited as the poorest county in the United States. There are about 310 reservations for 550 federally recognized tribes, corresponding to 2.3 percent of U.S. territory. Some tribes have several reservations, others share reservations, while still others have none. These reservations were only "leased" to their occupants; the federal government held title to the land. That typically American aberration was invented by the U.S. Congress, which passed the Indian Appropriations Act in 1851, a law stipulating the creation of territories in Oklahoma specifically reserved for the relocated Amerindians.

FRANK LESLIE'S ILLUSTRATED NEWSPAPER

No. 1,480.—Vol. LVIII.] NEW YORK—FOR THE WEEK ENDING MARCH 15, 1884. [PRICE, 10 CENTS.

EDUCATING THE INDIANS.—A FEMALE PUPIL OF THE GOVERNMENT SCHOOL AT CARLISLE VISITS HER HOME AT PINE RIDGE AGENCY.—FROM A SKETCH BY A CORRESPONDING ARTIST.—SEE PAGE 59.

The benefits of a mainstreamed education, personified by a student returning to the Pine Ridge Reservation from a government school. Engraving from *Frank Leslie's Illustrated*, 1884.

Pueblo women offering their crafts at the Saint Louis Universal Exposition.
Photograph by William H. Rau, 1904.

In the 1860s President Ulysses S. Grant (1822–1885), anticipating Joseph Stalin—who moved the people of the Soviet Union around like pawns on a chessboard—displaced tribes from their ancestral lands to distant reservations. "Indian reservation" seems a weak expression to designate the punishment to which these peoples were subjected. At the time, however, Grant declared he was conducting a peace policy that was supposed to quell conflicts between settlers and the tribes. Immediately afterward, that general-turned-president asked the Society of Friends (Quakers) to teach Christianity to the indigenous peoples in order to prepare them for civilization. After the Indian Wars and the defeat at Little Bighorn (June 25–26, 1876), Grant's policy was considered a failure, and the religious organizations withdrew. The original peoples of North America were in their death throes; it was the twilight of the civilizations of the bison, the reindeer, the salmon, and the thunderbird. The din of the iron horse's pistons and rods drowned out the howl of coyotes on the blood-soaked lands of the Far West. During this feverish period, new religions also arose, the final consolation for the misfortunes of the time and the failures of the ancient gods. The Ghost Dance, founded by the Paiute prophet Wovoka and adopted by the defeated Sioux, did not save the Amerindians, though it impressed crowds from the sprawling cities in the East.

By 1871 almost all the tribes in the United States had signed treaties that forced them to give up their lands in exchange for reservations and government benefits. But in 1887 the federal government once again changed its policy, pulling the Dawes Act out of its military cap. The avowed aim of the law was to turn every Native American into a landowner and farmer, encouraging integration into the new U.S. society. It no longer stipulated allocating one territory per tribe but rather dividing the territories into small parcels intended for individuals. The result: 136 million acres of reservation land were divided into small units, usually less than twenty-five acres, and given to settlers as well as Native American farmers. Ultimately, the tribes were robbed, legally or illegally, of wide-open spaces. It was not until 1934 that the Indian Reorganization Act put an end to the parcelization of lands and recognized the right to autonomy of Amerindian tribes. Those that accepted the new treaty were reorganized, so that they could purchase their own reservation lands.

A glimpse of the Mescalero Apache Reservation in New Mexico. Photograph by Arthur Rothstein, c. 1930.

Ten years later, in 1944, came a new change: the federal government's Indian Termination Policy put an end to the special status of Amerindians and sought to assimilate them into the larger society. The government declared it no longer recognized the sovereignty of the tribes. Henceforth, the indigenous peoples were citizens like everyone else, subject to federal laws and required to pay taxes. The new law was supposed to reduce their dependence on the Bureau of Indian Affairs, which had demonstrated its disastrous mismanagement of the reservations

President Calvin Coolidge receives a delegation of Comanche at the White House, 1928.

and its corruption. In 1953 Congress passed a law that abolished the special status of the reservations, making these territories subject to federal law. After World War II, successive U.S. administrations encouraged migration from the reservations to the cities and sought to dissolve the tribes. More than a hundred tribes lost their official status at the time. Simultaneously, the cleared territories were sold to non-Indians. In the 1970s, another policy took shape, supposedly favoring the protective role of the federal government by increasing tribal participation in local governance. The effect was to transfer Indian Affairs to the states, which had long sought to control tribal lands and resources.

Ultimately, the reservations did not remain on the fringes of the changing world. In 1979 the Seminole tribe in Florida was the first to open a casino on its reservation. After a few skirmishes between the tribes and the U.S. justice system, the Indian Gaming Regulatory Act was passed by Congress in 1988. It recognizes their right to offer gambling on their land and to build hotel complexes there. Let a thousand Las Vegases bloom! Combined with tourism, that activity, with its attendant corruption, has now become of major importance for the economies of certain tribes. It is common knowledge that law enforcement on reservations is not an FBI priority. It is estimated that, of the 2.5 million Amerindians, 1 million lived on reservations in 2012.

Left: Did they miss the train for modernity? Photograph by Leslie Jones, 1930.

Opposite: Chewing gum and a Wyandot headdress for a young Plains Assiniboine boy. Photograph by Burt Glinn, 1954.

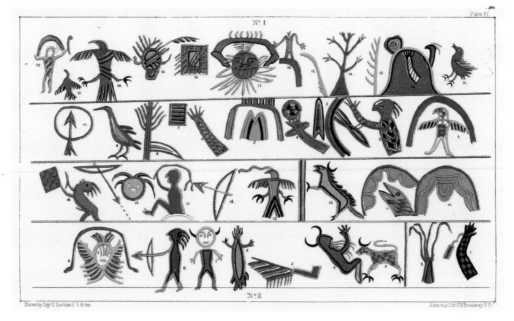

Notation of adventures from an Ojibwe cosmological chant. Painting on a birch plank, recopied by Henry Schoolcraft and Seth Eastman, 1851.

THE MIGHTY PENS OF AMERINDIAN WOMEN

In the nineteenth century—which saw the conquest of the continent and moves toward the eradication of its peoples (or ethnocide, to put it bluntly)—several remarkable Amerindian and Métis women found a way to express themselves, to educate themselves in mainstream culture, and to seize the adversary's weapons to make their own mark in the historical record. The first Amerindian woman writer was undoubtedly Jane Johnston Schoolcraft (1800–1842). Her Ojibwe name was Bamewawagezhikaquay, which means "the sound the stars make rushing through the sky." That is also the title of her book, which was not published until 2006. The granddaughter of an Ojibwe chief, she was inculcated in her culture by her mother, while her father, John Johnston (1762–1828), an Irish immigrant who became a trapper, taught her Anglophone literature. She lived a large part of her life in Sault Ste. Marie, Michigan, writing poems and stories in English about Ojibwe culture. She also translated songs from Ojibwe into English.

It was in Michigan that she met Henry Schoolcraft (1793–1864), known both as a geographer (he explored the Ozark Mountains and conducted an expedition to the sources of the Mississippi in 1832) and as the author of pioneering studies on Amerindian cultures. The fearless Schoolcraft, appointed to be an Indian agent at Fort Brady in Michigan in 1823, wasted no time in marrying the young poet. In 1826–27 Henry Schoolcraft brought out a handwritten magazine, *The Literary Voyager,* which included prose and poetry by his wife. He subsequently earned a certain renown thanks to his publications on the Amerindians, and especially on Ojibwe culture based on information provided to him by his wife and her family. Henry Schoolcraft's publications were the principal source of information for the poet Henry Wadsworth Longfellow (1807–1882) in composing his famous *Song of Hiawatha* (1855). That tragic love story between the Mohawk chief Hiawatha and the beautiful Minnehaha, the Amerindian Romeo and Juliet, caused a stir in its time.

The Schoolcrafts had four children. One of them died at the age of two, and Jane Johnston Schoolcraft expressed her sorrow by writing several poems on the subject. Her works were forgotten until 1962, when Philip P. Mason republished *The Literary Voyager* comprising her texts. Then, in 2006, Robert Dale Parker brought out her collected works in *The Sound the Stars Make Rushing through the Sky.*

Henry Schoolcraft was not unique: one of his friends, Brigadier General Seth Eastman (1808–1875), spent the better part of his life portraying the daily activities of tribes in delicate watercolors and pastels. It was he who illustrated the six volumes of Henry Schoolcraft's opus on the Amerindians. In 1830 Eastman, at

Sioux crossing a river. Painting by Seth Eastman, c. 1850.

the time a second lieutenant fresh out of West Point, was stationed to Fort Snelling, Minnesota, where he met his first wife, Wakaninajiwin, daughter of the Sioux chief Cloudman. She was fifteen at the time. They had a daughter, Mary. Eastman became a topographer in Florida, took part in the war against the Seminole, then crisscrossed the West painting everyday life. Less well known than George Catlin, the other painter of indigenous peoples and the first to paint Amerindian tribes "in nature," Eastman's art, produced just before the advent of photography, attests to an empathetic view of his subjects.

Sarah Winnemucca (c. 1844–1891) is the second Amerindian woman, after Sacagawea, to be honored with a bronze statue at the National Statuary Hall in the U.S. Capitol. She published the first autoethnography book in history, opened her own school, and gave lectures throughout the country—and, it should be added, was a valiant fighter for the rights of her people. Winnemucca was a Paiute from Nevada, daughter of Chief Old Winnemucca. While still a child, she learned English through contact with the families of settlers. She and her sister were enrolled in school but were forced out after a month, at the request of the other children's parents. A position as a domestic allowed her to perfect her English. In 1858, when the Paiute War broke out, Winnemucca left for the Pyramid Lake Reservation in Nevada with those of her people who had remained neutral. The new agent appointed in 1876 refused to pay the wages of the Paiute employed as agricultural workers. Winnemucca demanded that justice be done. With the assistance of General Howard, she also endeavored to secure the surrender of her father and his supporters, who had joined the rebel camp of Chief Buffalo Horn.

In 1879 Winnemucca went to Washington to plead with Secretary of the Interior Carl Schurz (1829–1907) for the right of the Paiute to live on the Malheur Reservation, the aptly named reservation in Oregon (*malheur* means "misfortune" or "unhappiness" in French). The reservation, established in 1872, would thus have concentrated—that is the right word—all the roaming tribes. In spite of her efforts, the federal employees at Indian Affairs relocated five hundred defeated Paiute warriors to the Yakama Reservation in Washington state, where they would suffer the worst privations. In 1883 Winnemucca went on a lecture tour, pleading for the rights of indigenous peoples and denouncing the misappropriations of the agents at the Bureau of Indian Affairs. She then published the book that would make her famous: *Life among the Piutes: Their Wrongs and Claims,* in which

Sarah Winnemucca, the first Amerindian woman to have published a book, *Life among the Piutes: Their Wrongs and Claims* (1883).

Group of Dakota women with their children; uprooted by the wars, they took refuge in a Catholic mission. Photograph by David Frances Barry, c. 1880.

she describes the first contacts between her people and the European explorers and settlers. During a meeting with Winnemucca, Senator Henry L. Dawes (1816–1903) succeeded in convincing her of the merit of his program to privatize Amerindian lands. Within a few years, settlers had completely taken over Malheur, and Winnemucca had to abandon her plan to resettle her people there. Having returned to Nevada in 1888, she founded a private school for Amerindian children, but she had to close it after the passage of the Dawes Act, which imposed English as the language of instruction. Winnemucca died of tuberculosis three years later.

Helen Hunt Jackson (1830–1885) was not born an Amerindian, but she made a name for herself with *Ramona* (1884), her novel about the California Indians. Outraged by what she was learning of the conduct of government agents toward them, Jackson became an activist. She began to do field investigations, circulate petitions, collect donations, and write letters to the *New York Times* on their behalf. A prolific writer, she had heated exchanges with representatives of the federal government

Helen Hunt Jackson, author of *Ramona*, a novel that would raise awareness of the Amerindian cause among a large readership.

Assimilation: learning to stand in line, c. 1890.

Mixing in the new West. A teacher, children, and Amerindian women intermingle on the Pine Ridge Reservation, c. 1890.

regarding the injustices done to the indigenous peoples. She revealed the blatant violation of treaties and the way that unscrupulous agents, officers, and settlers were encroaching on and stealing Amerindian lands. In 1881 Jackson published a pamphlet, *A Century of Dishonour,* which demanded significant reforms in government policy toward Amerindians. She sent a copy to every member of Congress with an admonition printed in red on the cover: "Look upon your hands: they are stained with the blood of your relations." But to no avail.

Jackson then decided to write a novel, *Ramona,* which would describe the experience of the Amerindians "in a way to move people's hearts." Inspired by *Uncle Tom's Cabin* (1852), written by her friend Harriet Beecher Stowe (1811–1896) years earlier, she confided: "If I can do one hundredth part for the Indian that Mrs. Stowe did for the Negro, I will be thankful." *Ramona* relates in simple language the life of an orphaned mixed-race girl raised in California's Spanish society and the life of her Amerindian husband, Alessandro. Jackson's novel, published in 1884, raised the awareness of some Americans to the ethnocide being perpetrated in the land of freedom.

Ignatia Broker (1919–1987), an Ojibwe born on the White Earth Reservation in Minnesota, was educated at the Wahpeton Indian School in North Dakota. Broker founded the Minnesota Historical Society and worked throughout her life to educate the general public about their Amerindian brothers and sisters. She left behind a book, *Night Flying Woman* (1983), which forcefully recounts the fateful confrontation between the rich traditions of her people of the forest and the desecration of the European invaders.

STOLEN WOMEN

U.S. history is abuzz with accounts of settler women held captive by Amerindians. Think of John Ford's sublime *The Searchers* (1956), in which Natalie Wood, the daughter of pioneers kidnapped by the Comanche, is the object of pursuit by the cynical bounty hunter John Wayne. The fantasy of the abducted girl who becomes the chief's wife and is recovered years later despite her protests and forcibly returned to the mainstream community is rooted in reality. That myth also tells of the call of Gitche Manitou (the Great Spirit) and the appeal of Amerindian life. North American history is a somber patchwork of interrelations. Several settler women who were kidnapped by Amerindians and lived among them for all or part of their lives left behind personal accounts. The captivity narrative is in fact an American literary genre in its own right.

The first was written by Mary Rowlandson (c. 1637–1711), a New England Puritan kidnapped with her three children by the Algonquian during King Philip's War, in 1675. She remained a prisoner for eleven weeks, before being ransomed. Rowlandson could then return to Princeton with her two surviving children. Her story, *The Sovereignty and Goodness of God: Being a Narrative of the Captivity and Restoration of Mrs. Mary Rowlandson,* recounts her ordeals and the brutality and bestiality of her abductors, who, it should be noted, did not rape her. Rowlandson also confides how she survived thanks to her skills as a seamstress, which were appreciated by her captors. They often moved their camp to escape their pursuers. Her book quickly became popular and united Puritan society in a widespread fear of the other.

Mary Jemison (1743–1833), taken in 1755 at the age of twelve by the Seneca in Pennsylvania, became a member of the tribe and remained one. Adopted by the family of the chief, she lived among them until her death in 1833. She is one of the rare women who, given the opportunity to return to live among her people,

Right: Frontispiece for Mary Rowlandson's captivity narrative.

Far right: Cynthia Ann Parker, the blue-eyed Comanche, mother of the rebel chief Quanah Parker.

MARY BEING ARRAYED IN INDIAN COSTUME.

Mary Rowlandson's captivity story was told to terrify children. Engraving from a nineteenth-century edition.

chose to end her days with her adoptive family. Jemison was eighty when she first met James Seaver, a former English minister, and confided her memories to him. He retranscribed them in a beautiful book for children: *A Narrative of the Life of Mrs. Mary Jemison.*

Cynthia Ann Parker (1827–1870), mother of the last Comanche chief, Quanah Parker (c. 1845–1911), knew the heartbreak of living in two irreconcilable worlds. In 1836, during a raid in Texas, Comanche warriors captured several women and children. One of the little girls was Cynthia Ann, ten years old at the time. She adapted well to Comanche life and, when she became an adolescent, married her kidnapper, Peta Nocono (1820–1864), whom she loved. In 1845 she gave birth to Quanah, who would become the last resistance leader of his people. In 1860, while her husband and his companions were out hunting, Texas Rangers attacked the Comanche village, captured "the blue-eyed Comanche," and returned her to her family. After two attempts to escape and rejoin the Comanche, the young woman allowed herself to die of starvation and grief.

Sarah E. Wakefield's *Six Weeks in the Sioux Tepees: A Narrative of Indian Captivity* tells how the author was abducted with her two children by the Santee Sioux during the uprising in Minnesota in 1862. That book still brings tears to the eyes of readers in the American heartland.

WOMEN WARRIORS

Amerindian women enjoyed physical rites and devoted themselves to various sports, such as lacrosse and running. Some learned hunting skills. The existence of women war chiefs was noted by the first colonists in the seventeenth century. In the Indian Wars of the nineteenth century, settlers had to contend with Amerindian women who gloriously resisted the invasions. The Cheyenne have not forgotten Buffalo Calf Road Woman (1850–1878), who saved her wounded brother at the Battle of the Rosebud in 1876, then fought alongside her husband at Little Bighorn: they say she threw General Custer off his horse. Ehyophsta ("yellow-haired woman" in Cheyenne) was a member of a secret women's society. She fought at the

Opposite: Some Cheyenne women were formidable warriors, such as Buffalo Calf Road Woman. Photograph by Edward S. Curtis, 1910.

Lozen and Dahteste (second row, right), prisoners with Geronimo and Naiche, await their departure for a penitentiary in Florida, 1886.

Two proud riders from the Flathead tribe on the Plains. Photograph by Edward H. Boos, c. 1905.

Battle of Beecher Island and against the Shoshone in 1868 and was one of the last Cheyenne to surrender. She died in 1915.

Two Apache women warriors also left a mark on their era. Dahteste (c. 1860–1955) rode alongside Cochise (1812–1874) with her family when she was just a child. She fought with Geronimo (1829–1909) and played a key role as an interpreter in negotiating the surrender to the U.S. cavalry. After spending eight years imprisoned in Florida, Dahteste was sent to a military prison at Fort Sill, Oklahoma, where she remained for nineteen years. Upon her release, she went to live on the Mescalero Apache Reservation and died at an advanced age, her unwavering character intact.

Lozen (1840–1887), sister of Victorio, the Chiricahua Apache chief, accompanied prestigious Apache warriors such as Geronimo, Mangas Coloradas, and Nana on many raids against the Mexicans and Americans. According to legend, she used her shamanic powers to learn of the enemy's movements. Lozen, still venerated by the Apache for her courage, endurance, and skill, possessed the strength of a man and acted as a shield to defend her people. Held prisoner at Mount Vernon Barracks in Alabama after Geronimo's surrender, she died of tuberculosis in 1887.

Opposite: Amerindian women left behind the memory of their indomitable courage, like this Brulé from the Lakota group. Photograph by Edward S. Curtis, 1907.

The Education of Amerindian Children

> Kill the Indian . . . and save the man.
>
> —Captain Richard Henry Pratt (1840–1924)

The Carlisle Indian Industrial School in Pennsylvania, founded by U.S. Army captain Richard Henry Pratt in 1879, became the model for dozens of other tribal schools established across the country by the Bureau of Indian Affairs. Pratt professed "assimilation through total immersion," a system he had developed at a Florida penitentiary. The officer and pedagogue made his position clear in an 1892 speech. "A great general has said that the only good Indian is a dead one. In a sense, I agree with the sentiment, but only in this: that all the Indian there is in the race should be dead. Kill the Indian in him and save the man." His attitude speaks for itself about the reception these schoolchildren would receive.

Federal legislation required that Amerindian children be educated based on the mainstream style with catechization, baseball, household chores, farmwork. With the creation of the Carlisle Indian Industrial School, the U.S. government organized a plan for true cultural erasure, the separation of children from their families and confinement to "Indian boarding schools." Parents were supposed to willingly send their children to school, but the U.S. Army often used force to fill the quotas assigned to the reservations. At the time, the authorities assumed that all indigenous customs were harmful and that only those of the mainstream culture led to civilization. Coercion began with the language: students were punished for speaking their native tongue. The goal was to obliterate every trace of Indianness in them.

Above: Portrait of three young students from the Carlisle Indian Industrial School, c. 1900.

Opposite: Little girls march toward progress at the Sheldon Jackson College in Alaska, 1900.

Young Chiricahua Apache upon their arrival at the Carlisle Indian
Industrial School. Photograph by M. E. Frye, 1886.

"The white man had concluded that the only way to save Indians was to destroy them, that the last great Indian war should be waged against children. They
were coming for the children," writes David Wallace Adams in his *Education for
Extinction: American Indians and the Boarding School Experience, 1875–1928* (1995).
Recent research has shown, however, that the U.S. government obtained scant results. In *Education beyond the Mesas: Hopi Students at Sherman Institute, 1902–1929*
(2010), the historian Matthew Sakiestewa Gilbert describes how Hopi students
were able to resist acculturation and get the most out of the forced education they
received. The United States won many battles, but it lost that last war: the tribes
were coming back to life.

The historian Clyde Ellis notes in a chapter of *Boarding School Blues* (2006):
"A funny thing happened on the way to assimilation. . . . The schools became
places where the construction of identity was deeply contested, where time and
time again Indian people proved more receptive to learning and more resilient in
culturally contextualizing that learning than policy makers ever imagined." In
France, many historical nationalist leaders including Ho Chi Minh, Habib Bour-
guiba, and Ferhat Abbas were trained in the Republic's schools. A similar process
continues even now in the United States, as evidenced by the resurgence of Native
American identity.

Young Chiricahua Apache, four months after their arrival at the Carlisle Indian Industrial School. Photograph by John N. Choate, 1886.

The assimilation of Amerindians began at a very young age, c. 1880.

Start of the school year at the Carlisle Indian Industrial School, c. 1900.

Pages 174–75: English lesson, theme of the day: the chair, 1901.

Left: Zitkala-Ša, or Red Bird, artist, woman of letters, and activist, born a Sioux. Photograph by Gertrude Käsebier, 1898.

ATTEMPTS AT ASSIMILATION

Zitkala-Ša (1876–1938), "Red Bird" in the Sioux language—also known as Gertrude Simmons Bonnin, the name given to her by the missionaries—writes in *The School Days of an Indian Girl* (1900): "The first day [of school] was a bitter-cold one.... My friend Judéwin knew a few words of English; and she had overheard the paleface woman talk about cutting our long, heavy hair. Our mothers had taught us that only unskilled warriors who were captured had their hair shingled by the enemy. Among our people, short hair was worn by mourners, and shingled hair by cowards! ... I cried aloud, shaking my head all the while until I felt the cold blades of the scissors against my neck, and heard them gnaw off one of my thick braids. Then I lost my spirit. Since the day I was taken from my mother I had suffered extreme indignities. People had stared at me. I had been tossed about in the air like a puppet. And now my long hair was shingled like a coward's! In my anguish I moaned for my mother, but no one came to comfort me. Not a soul reasoned quietly with me, as my own mother used to do, for now I was only one of many little animals driven by a herder."

Zitkala-Ša, born on the Yankton Indian Reservation in South Dakota in 1867, was taken by missionaries to White's Manual Labor Institute in Wabash, Indiana, at the age of eight. To escape her fate as a cleaning woman, she decided to educate herself and—an extraordinary achievement for the time—earned a degree from Earlham College in Richmond, Indiana. "For the white man's papers [the diplomas that would allow her to teach in the Indian schools], I had given up my faith in the Great Spirit. For these same papers I had forgotten the healing in trees and brooks. On account of my mother's simple view of life, and my lack of any, I gave her up, also. I made no friends among the race of people I loathed." And she notes: "In this fashion many [white visitors] have passed idly through the Indian schools during the last decade, afterward to boast of their charity to the North American Indian. But few there are who have paused to question whether real life or long-lasting death lies beneath this semblance of civilization."

Zitkala-Ša is a noble figure from the Belle Epoque. Her most widely read book, *American Indian Stories* (1921), is a collection of writings about her traditional childhood: living in a tepee, running through the tall grass in buckskin and moccasins. Of her mother, she says, "She taught me no fear save that of intruding myself upon others." Then, by contrast, she tells of her education in boarding schools, where she learned to speak, read, and write English, far from her mother and culture. We discover her heartbreak at being torn from the free and harmonious life of a little Sioux girl on the western prairies, loved and respected by her people, and taken to the hard, cruel life imposed on Amerindian children in the assimilation schools. Zitkala-Ša learned to play the piano and the violin, became a musician, and played with the New England Conservatory of Music from 1897 to 1899. She composed the songs for *The Sun Dance,* an opera performed by a troupe from the Ute Reservation to acclaim in Utah in 1913 and in New York in 1938.

Portrait of Zitkala-Ša.
Photograph by Gertrude
Käsebier, 1898.

Sewing class to prepare young Amerindian girls to take their places
on the production line, c. 1900.

She also continued to write. Her texts were published in *Harper's Magazine*
and *Atlantic Monthly,* then in the *American Indian Magazine,* for which she served
as editor in chief from 1918 to 1920. In 1919 she published "An Indian Praying on
a Hilltop," a return to her origins. "Great Spirit, for the superb gift of individual
consciousness, I offer thanks with over-flowing heart! For thy great law, protect-
ing my place in the spaces hung with the myriad stars, sun, moon, and earth, I offer thanks with my soul! Along my trail through the wilderness, dreadful dreams
overtake me by night and day; and I fear lest destruction make an end of me.
Thy power awakens me! Then, oh then, I rejoice in the spiritual realization that
earthly disaster cannot kill my spirit. I thank thee for awakening me! Poor in a
land of plenty; sick and weary of earth,—these are the terrors of my dreams both
night and day. Great Spirit I thank thee for awakening me! None can rob me of
thee! And the gift of conscious life,—in spirit! While upon the hilltop, I am pray-

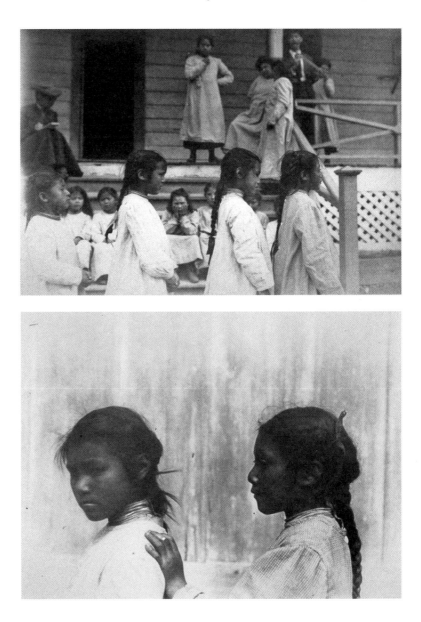

Students from Sonora, California, photographed by the ethnologist Alfred L. Kroeber in 1907, at about the same time that he met Ishi, the "last wild Indian," whom he protected and studied.

ing, I feel thy presence near. My strength is renewed like the eagle's. New courage brings its vision. I see the dawn of justice to the Indian, even upon earth; and now, Great Spirit, my heart is full of Joy!" Zitkala-Ša published many polemics (notably, in 1902, "Why I Am a Pagan" in *Atlantic Monthly* and "A Warrior's Daughter" in *Everybody's Magazine*) and, having become a political activist, in 1926 founded the National Council of American Indians to fight for civil rights, serving as its president until her death in 1938.

The "civilizing" effect of Home Economics: a sewing class at the Bismarck Indian School, North Dakota, 1909.

BROKEN SPIRITS

"Education in the white man's world is enriching and essential to economic success, but it need not mean the giving up of our proud Pima heritage," wrote Anna Moore Shaw (1898–1976), another Amerindian woman who has left us her autobiography. *A Pima Past* (1974) recounts her experience as a student at Phoenix Indian High School in the early twentieth century: "I worked in the dining room, washing dishes and scrubbing floors. If we were not finished when the 8:00 a.m. whistle sounded, the dining room matron would go around strapping us while we were still on our hands and knees." One of the popular slogans at the school was: "Be a Phoenix student not a reservation bum."

Here is the credo of Wellington Rich, superintendent of the Phoenix Indian High School (1893): "In order to civilize, to make good citizens of Indian youth, it is absolutely necessary that they be inspired with a strong desire for better homes, better food, better clothing, etc., than they enjoy in their natural state, and that they be qualified to obtain these things by their own exertions." In actuality, capitalist logic condemned legions of these children to the most menial work, to their misfortune.

In 1928 the U.S. government and the Rockefeller Foundation commissioned an investigation into the living conditions of Amerindians across the country. Published as the Meriam Report, it found that the infectious diseases widespread in Indian schools could be attributed to malnutrition, poor sanitary conditions, and student exhaustion. The investigation determined that the mortality rate of the students was six times higher than that of other ethnic groups. Despite these well-documented facts, Indian boarding schools proliferated until the 1970s. It is estimated that, from 1879 on, hundreds of thousands of Amerindian children passed through these schools. The rise of pan-Indian activism, the repeated complaints by tribal nations about these schools, and studies such as the Kennedy Report (1969) and the National Study of American Indian Education (1971) led

Home Economics class at the Carlisle School. Photograph by Frances Benjamin Johnston, 1901.

in 1975 to the passage of the Indian Self-Determination and Education Assistance Act, which allowed the decentralization of indigenous students to schools of their choice. As a result, most of the Indian schools closed in the 1980s and 1990s, for lack of backers.

Civics instruction: they were already saying that work makes you free. Photograph by Frances Benjamin Johnston, 1901.

8

Origins of Modern Mass Entertainment

FETISHISM AND ALIENATION

At roughly the same time that the push to erase Amerindian cultures was underway in the Indian boarding schools, that same heritage was being incorporated into the lore of the United States and the mythology of the West. Modern mass entertainment had its thunderous debut in the young United States of the late nineteenth century. Following the Civil War (1861–65), with the rise of cities and industry, the appetite of the crowd for the new and sensational was satisfied by the press. Front pages of newspapers trumpeted current events. Cheap, large-circulation books fed the mythology of the conquest of the West. Spectacles became the pinnacle of entertainment, and the people were subjected to their edifying fantasies. Vaudeville acts played at fairs, with larger-than-life spectaculars featuring fire-eaters and bear tamers. The rare, the odd, and the curious could be found at P.T. Barnum's circus, established in 1871. Under a big top accommodating ten thousand people, that first circus offered the public George Washington's supposed childhood nurse, Tom Thumb, and a sea serpent.

The display of the Hottentot Venus (1789–1815) had paved the way for the idea of exhibiting exotic peoples in cages. Carl Hagenbeck (1844–1913), director of the Hamburg Zoo, was the first to do just that by exhibiting Samoan and "Laplander" (Sami) populations in Germany in 1874. These human zoos provided Europeans with their first contact with otherness—safely behind barriers. Albert Geoffroy Saint-Hilaire gave his scientific backing to these "ethnological

Above: Buffalo Bill posing at the center of his band of Indians for the Wild West Show, 1908.

Opposite: Esther Eneutseak, in the Eskimo Village of the Saint Louis Universal Exposition. Photograph by Emme and Mayme Gerhard, 1904.

Omaha people exhibited at
the Jardin d'Acclimatation
in Paris, 1889.

spectacles," displaying "Eskimos" and Nubians at the Jardin d'Acclimatation
in Paris in 1877. The Expositions Universelles in Paris in 1878 and 1889 were not
immune to the inclination: four hundred indigenous extras were exhibited in
African, Kanak, or Annamite villages behind fences and gates. These populations
were put on stage to excite the curiosity of "civilized" people and to shore up the
superiority of European spectators, who could observe at their leisure the reified
bodies of the Other.

BUFFALO BILL

William Frederick Cody, known as Buffalo Bill (1846–1917), went to Paris with
his band of Amerindian performers for the first time in 1889 and naturally found
his place at the Jardin d'Acclimatation. In 1905 his cavalry paraded at the foot of
the Eiffel Tower before three million Parisians. Buffalo Bill's Wild West had become the standard of a popular American entertainment that would spread
around the world.

The rise of the obscure bison hunter William Cody to the status of national
and international hero was the doing of journalist Ned Buntline (c. 1821–1886). In
1869, at a lecture delivered to a temperance society in Nebraska, Buntline, a prolific
liar and inveterate alcoholic, met the man he would baptize, in the feature article
that made him famous, "Buffalo Bill, the King of the Border Men." In 1872 Buntline
put on a Broadway show, *Scouts of the Prairie*, starring Buffalo Bill, Texas Jack, an
Italian ballerina, and himself. The show was produced by James Gordon Bennett
Jr. (1841–1918), publisher of the *New York Herald*, who had just finessed his famous
scoop of having successfully sent Henry Morton Stanley in search of David Liv-
ingstone, the British explorer who had vanished in the heart of Africa and from

Right: Giuseppina Morlacchi, Italian dancer and actress. She played Buffalo Bill's Indian bride in *Scouts of the Prairie* in 1872.

Far right: Annie Oakley, one of the legendary women of the West, known for her sharpshooting. She joined the Wild West in 1885.

Nancy Columbia at the Universal Exposition in Saint Louis. Photograph by Emme and Mayme Gerhard, 1904. In October 1892 twelve Inuit families from Labrador were brought to the World's Fair in Chicago to perform at the Eskimo Village. Before the official opening of the exhibition, the women gave birth to four "World's Fair babies." During the fair, the group formed a new company to establish an independent Eskimo Village outside the fairgrounds. This was the beginning of their adventure. The Inuit appeared at eleven fairs and expositions, with the Barnum & Bailey Circus, at Coney Island, in Ocean Park, California, and then at the Exposition Universelle of Paris in 1889. They were ultimately hired by the Hollywood film studios in the 1910s. At the center of that story were two women: Esther Eneutseak (1877–1961), who took the Labrador group to Hollywood, and her daughter, Nancy Columbia (1893–1959), born in Chicago, who wrote and acted in the first Hollywood film with an Inuit cast, *The Way of the Eskimo* (1911), of which no trace remains. This was eleven years before Robert J. Flaherty's famous *Nanook of the North* (1922).

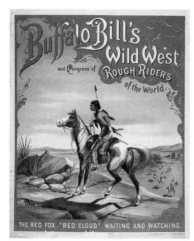

734. - Les Indiens de Buffalo à Paris. - G. I.

Poster of Buffalo Bill's Wild
West show. Illustration by
H. A. Thomas, 1893.

Performers from the Wild West
show in a bateau mouche in
Paris, 1905.

whom the world had been awaiting news. On Broadway, Cody acquired a taste for
the stage. In 1883, as "Buffalo Bill," he began to put on his Wild West show, taking
it on tour to enormous success.

It is said that, in its first two years, the show attracted ten million spectators and earned $100,000 in profits. It was the first time residents of the big cit-
ies in the East had been offered the emotion and adventure of the true West—but
without the risks. Amerindians were shown riding bareback in pursuit of bison,
dancing in front of their tepees, attacking a stagecoach. Cowboys broke mustangs
with their lassos. The rodeos amused viewers of all ages, as did the rifle-shooting
contests and knife throwers. The stars of the Wild West show achieved worldwide
renown. Annie Oakley (1860–1926) and Calamity Jane (1852–1903) fired their guns
to their hearts' content. Sitting Bull (c. 1831–1890) and his Sioux paraded in feathered headdresses in front of the U.S. citizenry. Reenactments of historical episodes
were very popular. The reconstruction of General Custer's death at the Battle of
Little Bighorn—supposedly a realistic representation of historical events—impressed the crowds. The Exposition Universelle of Paris in 1889 similarly had a
"living diorama" that reconstructed the last battle of the Amazons under King
Béhanzin (1845–1906) of Dahomey, who was defeated by the French in 1894.

These shows offered spectators representations of a history still being
made. The same process of distancing and appropriation was at work as in the
theater of classical antiquity. At a time when the West was being radically transformed, U.S. society put the indigenous world on display in museums or on the
stage, in an ultimate bid against the end of an era. On the one hand, anthropologists collected the dying voices of the last free indigenous peoples. On the other,
a circus rehabilitated and mythicized the old enemies of the United States before
they vanished. Until 1913, Buffalo Bill's Wild West would dazzle the whole world,
sowing the seeds of its romance and characters for Hollywood, which would then
cultivate them.

GEORGE CUSTER

George Custer (1839–1876) anticipated the importance of the media, if not his place in the drama later created by Buffalo Bill. Undoubtedly one of the first soldiers to take journalists along on his expeditions so that they could recount his exploits, he was himself—under the pseudonym "Nomad"—the author of the best seller *My Life on the Plains* (1874), written to his glory. The daring Captain Custer had attracted notice during the Civil War. From 1868 onward, he took part in the wars against the Cheyenne, winning notoriety for the massacre of women and children on the Washita River. In 1873 Custer was sent into Dakota Territory to protect a railroad line under construction against attacks from the Sioux.

The Northern Pacific Railway Company was attempting to connect Lake Superior to the Pacific Ocean via reservation lands, in defiance of the Treaty of Fort Laramie (1868) which guaranteed the integrity of said territories. Its chief financier, Jay Cooke (1821–1905), had borrowed a large amount of money and was obliged to attract settlers along his line to recoup his losses. Cooke appealed to the press. August Belmont's editorials in the *New York World* and those of James Gordon Bennett in the *New York Herald* set off a gold rush into sacred tribal lands. The Plains nations mustered their forces. Their incessant attacks on the railroad line construction sites shook investors' confidence, resulting in bankruptcy for the Northern Pacific and the panic of September 18, 1873, which obliged Wall Street to close its doors for ten days. Readers of the eastern press were kept informed live by telegraph. The holy alliance of military, business, and the media was set in place. The iron horse would advance westward.

In 1874 General Custer, leading twelve hundred soldiers, a hundred ten wagons, and three embedded journalists, penetrated the Black Hills of Dakota, a

Cavalry captain George Custer, fresh out of West Point, 1861.

Custer poses in front of a grizzly, killed during the expedition that would end in the Battle of Little Bighorn, 1874.

The presidential memorial at Mount Rushmore under construction. Photograph by Leslie Jones, 1931.

territory still untouched by settlement and the center of the world for the Sioux and Cheyenne. As anticipated, the expedition found gold. Custer and his friend Clement A. Lounsberry (1843–1926), founder of the *Bismarck Tribune,* had the scoop. Prospectors rushed to the Indian territories. Boomtowns such as Bismarck, Deadwood, and Hill City sprang up near the gold deposits. Custer City, created in August 1875 with six hundred residents, grew to ten thousand just nine months later. The Sioux and Cheyenne revolted against the "thieves' road," which desecrated their Black Hills sanctuary. On June 25, 1876, at the Battle of Little Bighorn, 285 "bluecoats" from General Custer's 7th Cavalry were killed by the Cheyenne under the command of Two Moons (1847–1917) and the Sioux led by Sitting Bull and Crazy Horse (1849–1877). The only journalist present, Mark Kellogg of the *Bismarck Herald,* was the first war correspondent to die in combat. It was a last stand for these tribes, who could no longer fend off the irresistible expansion.

During the same period, William Randolph Hearst (1863–1951), the newspaper magnate whom Orson Welles would take for his model in *Citizen Kane* (1941) and one of the proponents of the sensational journalism that would take hold, also made his fortune in the gold mines of the Black Hills.

Mount Rushmore, named after a New York attorney who passed through in 1885, happens to be the sacred mountain of Six Grandfathers in the spiritual pilgrimage of the Lakota recounted by Black Elk. The presence of the indigenous people in those South Dakota mountains is attested for at least the last eight thousand years. As such, when Mount Rushmore was turned into a presidential memorial, it was almost as if it were making matters absolutely clear, so that people would know to whom that region belonged. Sculptor Gutzon Borglum, a member of the Ku Klux Klan and the spur behind the idea of the presidential visages, was obsessed with an "American art" that would glorify the accomplishments of his country, in the heroic nationalist vein beloved of Mussolini, Hitler, and Stalin during the same period. From 1927 to 1941, the megalomaniacal sculptor used dynamite to carve out, on the face of Mount Rushmore, sixty-foot-tall profiles of four U.S. presidents: George Washington, Thomas Jefferson, Abraham Lincoln, and Theodore Roosevelt, "in commemoration of the foundation, preservation, and continental expansion of the United States." They are now part of the landscape, though some find that land art an offense to the indigenous people, at the very least.

Such state propaganda is no longer in season. Yet the mythology of America was forged under the big sky of the Far West.

The Wild West show at the Champ de Mars in Paris, 1905.

During what was known as the Belle Epoque, a few authentic Native American artists found expression and were snapped up by the insatiable ogre of show business. All Canadian schoolchildren know *The Song My Paddle Sings,* the poem by E. Pauline Johnson (1861–1913), aka Tekahionwake, born on a reservation in Ontario in 1861. That writer and artist, of Mohawk and English descent, is still known for her poetry celebrating the culture of the First Nations. Canada even devoted a postage stamp to her.

Te Ata (1895–1995)—"Morning Star" in Chickasaw—an actress and recounter of Indian folklore, was invited to the White

House by President Roosevelt in 1933. Te Ata wrote a number of books for children and, at the end of her long life, was named "Oklahoma's State Treasure." She can be seen performing in the film *God's Drum* (1971).

Florence Tsianina Evans, or Tsianina Redfeather, or Tsianina Blackstone (1882–1985), a Creek Cherokee from Oklahoma, had a bright career as a singer and dancer but is now largely forgotten.

9

American Indian Women in Hollywood

THE DREAM FACTORY WRITING HISTORY

Sacheen Littlefeather had her moment of glory at the Academy Awards ceremony in 1973, when Marlon Brando delegated the young actress, dressed in full Apache regalia, to denounce to the world the racist treatment Hollywood had inflicted on the Native Americans and to decline his Oscar as a gesture of solidarity with the American Indian Movement.

Yet things had started out well between the film industry in its infancy and the Amerindians it chose to portray. In *The Squaw Man* (Cecil B. DeMille, 1914), the first feature-length film made (in a barn) in Hollywood, the female lead was played by Red Wing, a Ho-Chunk born on a reservation in Nebraska. Educated at the Carlisle Indian Industrial School, Red Wing married James Young Deer, a Nanticoke actor for P.T. Barnum's circus. The couple was hired by the Pathé Frères movie studio in Jersey City; Young Deer became a producer, Red Wing an actress. *White Fawn's Devotion* (1910), the only silent film directed and performed by Native Americans to be preserved, showcases their work. The entertainers later went to California to make films about the (freshly minted) "Old West" in a more authentic environment. In those early days, Red Wing became the first Native American actress in the New World.

Sacheen Littlefeather at the Oscars, 1972.

Above: Elsa Martinelli in André De Toth's *Indian Fighter*, 1955.

Opposite: Audrey Hepburn in John Huston's *Unforgiven*, 1960.

Filming of Cecil B. DeMille's *The Squaw Man,* 1914.

ONCE UPON A TIME
IN THE WEST

But Brando would turn out to be in the right: the movie industry was slow to give feature roles to Native Americans. The story of the conquest of the West, told from the viewpoint of the victors, depicted the indigenous world in crude stereotypes— whooping savages in war paint, servile wives, or wily temptresses. In the first westerns, the Far West is only the setting for melodrama. Thomas H. Ince created the first Hollywood movie studio in 1911, with D. W. Griffith and Mack Sennett. These pioneers in assembly-line filmmaking invented a method of scripted film production which relied on a detailed scenario, the first incarnation of the story-boards and editing techniques used for modern films. Until 1918 the Triangle Film Corporation would make hundreds of mass-produced western dramas, imitating the success of Henry Ford's automobile production. The stories would be inspired by Buffalo Bill's Wild West, a model of popular entertainment at the time.

Hollywood codified a typology of western characters, which persisted through spaghetti westerns and into contemporary films, such as Quentin Tarantino's *Django Unchained* (2012). The situation was somewhat similar to that of Paris in the seventeenth century, when, it is said, the stock characters of Pont-Neuf street theater, such as Tabarin and Scaramouche, influenced Molière's classical comedy. In western saloons, you ran into the lonesome cowboy always ready for adventure, the good-time barmaid, the aging sheriff and the outlaw gang, the idealistic newspaperman and the snake oil peddler, the professional gambler and the Chinese cook, the determined homesteader and his virtuous bride. Cruel, scalp-hunting warriors, attacking anything on wheels—stagecoaches, wagon trains, the iron horse, all duly saved by the bluecoats—played a major role in this narrative.

The western genre became the stage where the history of *Homo americanus* played out. Every western deals with what are still burning issues in the United States: individualism, wide-open spaces, gun control, the democratic ideal and frontier justice, Christian virtues, and unapologetic opulence.

For a long time, the "Hollywood Indian woman" was simply part of the background. When she emerged from it, she turned out to be a dangerous siren to the frontiersman. In Hollywood it is unthinkable that a blonde woman should succumb to the charms of any brave, unless she has been kidnapped and ravaged. By contrast, the myth of the mountain man winning the heart of the beautiful "savage" justified the conquest of Amerindian territory. The stereotype of the chief's daughter who falls for the European hero, sacrifices herself for him, and dies as a result is a thread that runs from *The Squaw Man* to Richard Brooks's classic *The Last Hunt* (1956), where "the love between Stewart Granger and the Indian

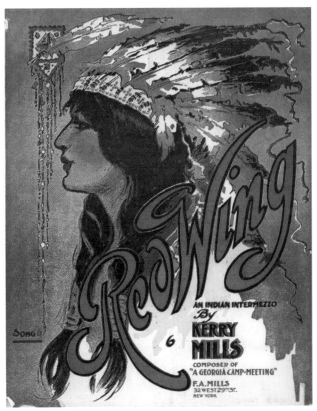

Above: Poster for Cecil B. DeMille's remake of *The Squaw Man*, 1931.

Right: Kerry Mills's Red Wing songbook, 1907.

In his remake of *The Squaw Man*, DeMille replaced Red Wing with the Mexican actress Lupe Vélez, 1931.

Debra Paget represents the conquest of a country of which one would be the explorer and the sole occupant," as Raymond Bellour writes in *Le Western* (1993). The founding myth of the Amerindian's assimilation into the settler world dates back to the legend of Pocahontas. It ends in marriage, with the children becoming the legitimate heirs to the riches of Native American land.

Ince's westerns show a certain empathy for the fate of the indigenous peoples. In *The Heart of an Indian* (1912), two mothers—one settler, the other Amerindian—are held hostage in a dual act of revenge and share the same fate. The Hollywood practice of having "Caucasian" actors in redface took hold. In *The Invaders* (Francis Ford, 1912), the role of the Sioux chief is played by Francis Ford himself, the elder brother of John Ford. And the pretty brunette Ann Little makes an improbable Native American. But Ince also cast his friend William Eagle Shirt, an actual Sioux, in several of his films. The extras for the first Hollywood westerns came from a group of Navajo with their camp in Malibu. They were on the payroll of the studio, and a bus took them to the surrounding hills for their days of stunt riding. In the realm of fantasy what did it matter that these Navajo were playing Sioux dressed in eagle feathers?

Griffith's first films still depicted Amerindians as sympathetic figures, as in *The Red Man's View* (1909), or victims, as in *The Massacre* (1914), which denounced the notorious General Custer without naming him. Griffith, "the father of film

Scene from *The Heart of an Indian*, a short film by Thomas H. Ince, 1912.

The world turned upside down: Linda Darnell as an Amerindian teaching Buffalo Bill (Joel McCrea) to read in William A. Wellman's film, 1944.

Right: Poster for Richard Brooks's *Last Hunt*, 1956.

Far right: Poster for *The Battle of Elderbush Gulch*, a short film by D. W. Griffith, 1913.

grammar," shot footage of the battlefield. Men on horseback pursue indigenous warriors. Under a pyramid of bodies, a hand moves; a couple and a child appear. The camera zooms in on that radiant American family emerging from a pile of corpses. An ambiguous happy ending—and cinema became a tragic art. But the racist orientation of the director of *The Birth of a Nation* (1915), which caused riots when it was shown in the northern states, found expression in *The Battle of Elderbush Gulch* (1913), where Griffith depicts crude, dog-eating Indians who devour the little settler heroine's puppies.

In Hollywood's golden age, the roles of African Americans were played by actors in blackface, as in *The Jazz Singer* (Alan Crosland, 1927), the first talkie. Likewise, actresses in redface played Indians.

INDIAN PRINCESSES, REELS OF FILM

Yvonne De Carlo was the Indian princess Wah-Tah in *The Deerslayer* (Lew Landers, 1943), and Linda Darnell played Dawn Starlight, who taught Buffalo Bill (Joel McCrea) to read in an excellent scene from William A. Wellman's film (*Buffalo Bill*, 1944). Audrey Hepburn is remembered for her role as a shamefaced Kiowa in John Huston's *Unforgiven* (1960). In *Broken Arrow* (Delmer Daves, 1950), Debra Paget, the only survivor of the massacre of her tribe, falls in love with James Stewart and sacrifices her life to save him. Many made-in-Hollywood Indian princesses have stayed with film lovers: Sara Montiel in *Run of the Arrow* (Samuel Fuller, 1957), Jean

Taming of the native woman, Hollywood style: Joel McCrea and Susan Cabot in Joseph M. Newman's *Fort Massacre,* 1958.

Peters in *Apache* (Robert Aldrich, 1954), Susan Cabot in *Fort Massacre* (Joseph M. Newman, 1958), Donna Reed in *The Far Horizons* (Rudolph Maté, 1955), Cyd Charisse in *The Wild North* (Andrew Marton, 1952), Elizabeth Threatt—who died too soon—in *The Big Sky* (Howard Hawks, 1952), and Elsa Martinelli frolicking with Kirk Douglas in a designer buckskin tunic in *The Indian Fighter* (André De Toth, 1955). Other "ethnic" roles went to Mexicans, such as Lupe Vélez in the remake of *The Squaw Man* (Cecil B. DeMille, 1931), Movita Castaneda in *Fort Apache* (John Ford, 1948) and *Wagon Master* (John Ford, 1950), María Elena Marqués as a Blackfoot married to the trapper played by Clark Gable in *Across the Wide Missouri* (William A. Wellman, 1951), Dolores del Rio in *Cheyenne Autumn* (John Ford, 1964); or to Caribbean actresses, such as Rita Moreno in *The Yellow Tomahawk* (Lesley Selander, 1954). Even Brando, in *One-Eyed Jacks* (1961), the only film—a western—that he directed, cast Mexican beauties Pina Pellicer and Katy Jurado in starring roles. His resentment about film's manipulation of national history must have come later.

Natalie Wood in one of her greatest roles in John Ford's *Searchers,* 1956.

Nonnative women in redface in the
1950s: Jean Peters in Robert Aldrich's
*Apache,*1954 (*below*), and María
Elena Marqués (*right*) in William A.
Wellman's *Across the Wide Missouri,* 1951.

It was not until the 1980s that Native American women would play their
own roles in Hollywood. Geraldine Keams, a Navajo actress, in *The Outlaw Josey
Wales* (Clint Eastwood, 1976), and Tantoo Cardinal, a Cree, in *Dances with Wolves*
(Kevin Costner, 1990), were the first Amerindian women seen on screen since
Red Wing. In 1950, however, Anthony Mann had used Native American men for
the secondary roles in *Devil's Doorway,* and Delmer Daves had done the same in
Broken Arrow.

Broken Arrow tells the true story of an idealistic postmaster in Arizona,
who, in the midst of the war against the Apache, goes off by himself to negotiate a
truce with Cochise in his mountain stronghold, so that the mail—symbol of civilization—can get through. In that memorable antiracist film, James Stewart falls in
love with Debra Paget, in the role of Sonseebrav the White Painted Lady—mother
of life, crowned in eagle down feathers—who will initiate him into the Amerindian world. Their love is symbolized by a pocket mirror in which each sees the
other both different and the same. The pacifist settler who becomes a tribal member for the love of a woman delivers a message of tolerance and humility, which is
answered only by the violence of the implacable fighters on both sides. That sub-
versive screenplay by Albert Maltz, one of the screenwriters on the Hollywood
blacklist during the McCarthy era, marked a turning point in the film industry.
The director, Delmer Daves, an expert in the habits and customs of the Navajo
and Hopi—having spent time on their reservations as an adolescent—filmed a few

brief ethnological sequences showing Apache in their daily lives, as well as dancing scenes, unique in the history of the western. In an interview published in *Amis américains* (*American Friends,* 1993; reissued 2008), Daves told Bertrand Tavernier: "I like *Broken Arrow* very much, because in that film I was able to show the Indian as a man of honor and principle, a human being and not a bloodthirsty savage. It was the first time he was shown speaking the way a civilized man would speak to his people, about their problems and future. The UN praised that film because it portrays a world where people in conflict respect one another. There were bastards among the whites, but also respectable types, just as there were fanatical Indians but also trustworthy men. After that, Hollywood stopped painting Indians as savages."

In the 1950s westerns began to take pity on the Native Americans. In the 1960s, their dignity would slowly be restored to them on film. That new empathetic view would reach its high point in *Cheyenne Autumn,* John Ford's last, elegiac western. A U.S. historian in the guise of filmmaker, Ford sought to film the saga of the conquest of the West beginning with *The Iron Horse* (1924), which featured eight hundred Pawnee, Cheyenne, and Sioux and thirteen thousand bison. Ford's filmography is emblematic of the evolution of the western. Before World War II, he depicted primitive and bloodthirsty Indians, in *Stagecoach* (1939) and in the beautiful historical film *Drums along the Mohawk* (1939), in which New England colonists Henry Fonda and Claudette Colbert face terrifying "red devils" during the Revolutionary War. In his trilogy on the cavalry, *Fort Apache* (1948), *She Wore a*

Dolores del Rio and Gilbert Roland in John Ford's *Cheyenne Autumn,* 1964.

Pina Pellicer and Marlon Brando in his *One-Eyed Jacks,* 1961.

Geraldine Keams and Clint Eastwood in his *Outlaw Josey Wales,* 1976.

Yellow Ribbon (1949), and *Rio Grande* (1950), anonymous Amerindians are still part of the natural wilderness that must be conquered in the interest of civilization. Then, from one film to the next until 1966, Ford would take a more sour and disenchanted view of the conquest of the West and the Indian Wars. The Manichaeism of his earlier days gave way to a reflection on the violence, racism, and tragedy suffered by the tribal nations. His artistic gifts having reached the height of perfection, he would deliver his last masterpieces, *The Searchers* (1956), *Two Rode Together* (1961), and *Cheyenne Autumn* (1964), which recount a less conventional history.

INDIAN LOVERS

Then, finally, came *Little Big Man* (Arthur Penn, 1970), which blew apart the legends of the West and pulled a few skeletons out of the American ideal's closet. It was the first western to mention the massacres the U.S. Army had perpetrated at Sand Creek, the Washita River, and Wounded Knee. And it was the first film to offer a new vision: the Amerindian world with a human face, humor and tragedy combined. *Little Big Man* dared say that Indians' integration equaled their decline. But though Chief Dan George, 121 years old in the film, honors the memory of the first Americans, it was an Asian actress, Aimée Eccles, not a Native American, who played Sunshine in that western where everyone speaks English.

Dustin Hoffman and Aimée Eccles in Arthur Penn's *Little Big Man*, 1970.

Nevertheless, the distance Hollywood has traveled can be measured by the different characterizations of Custer across time, from the chivalrous Errol Flynn in *They Died with Their Boots On* (Raoul Walsh, 1941) to the buffoonish Old Curly in *Little Big Man,* whose contempt for the tribes would lead him to disaster. In another famous western, *A Man Called Horse* (1970, Elliot Silverstein), the role of Running Deer, the Sioux chief's sister engaged to the protagonist, is played by Corinna Tsopei, the first Greek Miss Universe (1964). In the same era, oddly enough, the Mexican actor Anthony Quinn played Zorba the Greek in the film by that name (Mihalis Kakogiannis, 1964). And in *Jeremiah Johnson* (Sydney Pollack, 1972), the Crow chief's daughter, married to the trapper Robert Redford, is played by the actress Delle Bolton, who is also not the Indian she is supposed to be.

Since the 1990s and 2000s, Native American actors and directors have finally begun to find a place in show business. Some have become bankable. Could U.S. society be accepting its racial mix one step at a time? For Russell Means, the Lakota actor in *The Last of the Mohicans* (Michael Mann, 1992), *Natural Born Killers* (Oliver Stone, 1994), and *Into the West* (2005)—a longtime political activist who occupied Alcatraz in San Francisco Bay with the American Indian Movement in 1969—the fight was not over: "As Americans we have faced up to many social ills. Anti-Semitism, racism against blacks, oppression of women, and now it's time to face up to the Indian issue."

"Americans are overgrown children!" Europeans like to say, a statement based on the youth of the United States, the brevity of its history, which is lighter to bear than that of the Old World, and on its wide-open spaces, playgrounds for the pioneers. Such overgrown children must be constantly entertained: Disney creates a wonderful parallel world for them, and Hollywood gives them a clear conscience. From its beginnings, the movie industry has been the champion of the American way of life. From the start, Hollywood moguls knew how to amuse crowds with that magical new tool of worldwide distribution. The history of the conquest of the West was concocted, at best, as hagiography, at worst as foolish nonsense and lies. A few westerns, however, will remain in our memories as sources and traces of the wild frontier as we imagined it to be. Hollywood shaped an image of America being built under the big sky of the West, an image constitutive of the country's identity. It is Hollywood that wrote the history of America.

The Resistance of American Indian Women

A nation is not conquered until the hearts of its women are on the ground. Then it is finished no matter how brave its warriors or how strong their weapons.

—Cheyenne proverb

The legal concept of genocide, developed at the Nuremberg trials in 1946, refers to the deliberate physical extermination of a racial minority. But the term "genocide" was not adequate for ethnologists such as Robert Jaulin, who, in *La paix blanche* (*White Peace*, 1970), was the first to formulate the concept of ethnocide, the negation and destruction of a people's culture. Since then, the use of the term "ethnocide" has extended far beyond its point of origin. As Pierre Clastres, an eminent member of the French school of anthropology, explained: "Ethnocide, then, is the systematic destruction of modes of life and thought belonging to people different from those who undertake that destruction. In brief, genocide murders people's bodies, ethnocide kills their spirits. In the latter case, it is still death, but death of a different kind: immediate physical obliteration is not cultural eradication, which has long-deferred effects, depending on the oppressed minority's capacity to resist. No question here of choosing the lesser of two evils, the response being only too obvious: it is better to have less barbarism than more. That said, we need to reflect on the true meaning of ethnocide. It sees the Other in the same way genocide does: the Other is difference, granted, but above all, it is bad difference. The two attitudes diverge on the question of how difference is to be treated. The genocidal spirit, so to speak, wants to deny it pure and simple. The others are exterminated because they are absolutely evil. Ethnocide, by contrast, concedes the relativity of the evil in difference: others are bad, but they can be improved if they are constrained to transform themselves, until they become, if possible, identical

Above: Helen Fragua and her family in Albuquerque, New Mexico. Photograph by Michelle Vignes, 1980s.

Opposite: Alberta holds the sacred pipe on a march to Rapid City, South Dakota. Photograph by Michelle Vignes, 1980s.

Taos Pueblo, New Mexico. Photograph by Michelle Vignes, 1980s.

to the model being proposed or imposed on them. Genocide and ethnocide can be viewed as perverse forms, respectively, of pessimism and optimism." Clastres also invokes Claude Lévi-Strauss's *Race et histoire* (*Race and History*, 1952), in which the great anthropologist reminds us that the first indigenous island peoples to meet them wondered whether the newly arrived Spaniards were gods or men, whereas the Europeans inquired whether the indigenous peoples were human or animal in nature. That is the history of the Americas in a nutshell.

The conquerors of the New World attacked the indigenous peoples' territories and immediately afterward their souls. As in most cases of colonization, the missionaries followed the armed forces, when they did not precede them. And the propagators of the Christian faith excluded difference—paganism—by bringing with them the true faith, for the good of the "uncivilized." Another discourse, secular in this case, maintained that, for the native peoples to be integrated into society at the national level, they would have to abandon their traditions. Only assimilation would allow these minorities to participate fully in the development of the country and to enjoy its benefits. That hierarchical view of cultures still enjoys free rein. "Ethnocide is the suppression of cultural differences judged to be inferior and bad, the implementation of a plan to reduce the other to the same; the Indian is suppressed as other and reduced to the same as citizen," wrote Clastres.

AFFIRMATION OF LIFE

The nineteenth century ended with the twilight of the Amerindian world. The promised land of some became the lost paradise of others. Photos of Amerindians from that time deliver a message from a space-time that has vanished forever. We can only guess now at what stands behind their distant gazes, accustomed to vast horizons, and suddenly faced with the walls of "civilization."

The armed resistance to the invaders was carried out by warriors, often men. Cultural resistance, however, was and continues to be mounted often by women. From the twentieth century until our own time, Amerindian women have relentlessly stoked the fires of the Great Spirit, while affirming their dignity and vital force. The clash between the two worlds exterminated entire populations, and colonization pressed its advantage. But it did not manage altogether to break the tribal circle. We have seen that U.S.-style education failed to completely assimilate the First Nations. School instead taught them the adversary's language and showed them how to organize their resistance. It should also be acknowledged that U.S. universities have made it possible for several generations of Native Americans, women especially, to turn their learning to their advantage in an attempt to protect their peoples. In a modern extension of their traditional role, these educated women have become pedagogues, doctors, and ethnologists, lawyers struggling against the despoliation of their territories, political activists fighting for civic and ecological rights. Their natural authority has made them leaders of their violated people.

Wife of Chief Red Eagle. Photograph by Herbert E. French, 1947.

THE LITERARY RENAISSANCE
OF NATIVE AMERICAN WOMEN

In the 1970s an indigenous cultural resistance movement emerged and seized the modern means of communication. It is clear that the Native American oral tradition has adapted to Western written forms. That achievement has obviously had a salubrious effect on North American literature. The voices of American Indians had already enriched the treasury of humankind's tales and myths. Ethnological monographs and autobiographies by those who identified as Indians had been published by academic presses. But the new Native American literature leaves aside tribal themes and confronts contemporary mainstream American reality. A

Esther Martinez in Ohkay Owingeh, New Mexico.
Photograph by Michelle Vignes, 1980s.

Mother and her child at Taos Pueblo, New Mexico.
Photograph by Michelle Vignes, 1980s.

new generation is now finding expression. A "Native American Renaissance" is the term coined by the critic Kenneth Lincoln to describe this indigenous literary revival, whose origins he locates in N. Scott Momaday's *House Made of Dawn*, which won its author the Pulitzer Prize in 1969, and in James Welch's poetry collection *Riding the Earthboy 40* (1971).

Some of the strongest figures in this continuing literary and artistic renaissance are women. Native American or Métis poets, novelists, and essayists are published regularly and attract a great deal of notice. Anonymous, passive, subaltern? Women framed as silent in the myth of the West have left their reservations behind.

Appendix 1

The American Indian Renaissance

Polingaysi Qoyawayma, or Elizabeth Q. White (1892–1990), a Hopi, was born in Oraibi, Arizona. A rebel, she was torn between two cultures throughout her life. She was a Mennonite missionary for a while, then later developed an innovative and controversial pedagogy that was not accepted by her people for a long time. She was also a poet and potter and published an autobiography: *No Turning Back: A Hopi Indian Woman's Struggle to Live in Two Worlds* (1964).

Irene Stewart (b. 1907), born on the Navajo reservation near Canyon de Chelly in Arizona, was raised in traditional ways by a shaman father and a weaver mother. She graduated from the Albuquerque Indian School in 1929 and became a member of the Navajo Nation Council. Stewart recounted her life as a bilingual and bicultural Indian between two worlds in *A Voice in Her Tribe: A Navajo Woman's Own Story* (1981).

Mildred Imoch (En-Ohn or Laya-Bet) (1910–1997), a maker of traditional dolls, a teacher, and an Apache leader, was born in Fort Sill, Oklahoma, where her parents were imprisoned with Geronimo and the last Chiricahua fighters. A teacher in various Indian schools throughout her life, in 1976 she was chosen by the Apache tribe of Fort Sill to be the leader of their autonomous government, where she worked until the age of eighty-five.

Annie Dodge Wauneka (1910–1997), an influential member of the Navajo Nation Council, received the Medal of Freedom from President Lyndon B. Johnson in 1963 for her work in the fields of health and education.

Elizabeth Peratrovich (1911–1958), born into the Raven clan of the Tlingit Nation in the Pacific Northwest, was an important civil rights activist who worked for the passage of the Anti-Discrimination Act, which in 1945 banned "No Natives Allowed" signs in public places in Alaskan territory.

Ignatia Broker (1919–1987), an Ojibwe born on the White Earth Reservation in Minnesota, was educated at the Wahpeton Indian School in North Dakota. Founder of the Minnesota Indian Historical Society, she published innovative books, such as *Night Flying Woman* (1983), which tells of the fatal confrontation between the traditions of her forest people and the desecration by the European invaders. It is considered one of the first indigenous perspectives on American history.

Beatrice Medicine (1923–2005), an anthropologist and a professor at California State University, was a descendant of the Sihasapa and Miniconjou of the Lakota Sioux. She was one of the women of that nation who resisted cultural assimilation. In *The Native American Woman: A Perspective* (1978), Medicine published the results of her research on the role of women in Lakota culture in the face of changes to traditional life. She wrote of her dual identity in *Learning to Be an Anthropologist and Remaining "Native": Selected Writings* (2001).

Elizabeth Cook-Lynn (b. 1930) is a Lakota Creek Crow poet, essayist, and novelist, founder of the review *Wicazo Sa* (The Red Pencil) devoted to Native American studies. "Writing is an essential act of survival for contemporary American Indians. . . . The final responsibility of a writer like me . . . is to commit something to paper in the modern world which supports this inexhaustible legacy left by our ancestors." Born on a reservation in South Dakota in 1930, Cook-Lynn taught for a long time at the Women's Studies Center of Eastern Washington University, in support of the "cultural, historical, and political survival of Indian nations." Her trenchant views on tribal sovereignty gave rise to many controversies. The titles of her books say it all: *The Politics of Hallowed Ground: Wounded Knee and the Struggle for Indian Sovereignty*

(1999); *A Separate Country: Postcoloniality and American Indian Nations* (2012). In an autobiographical essay excerpted from the collection *I Tell You Now,* Cook-Lynn explains how her sense of being excluded from American society and her discovery that her people's history was being denied in American textbooks turned to anger and compelled her to write: "Writing, for me, then, is an act of defiance born of the need to survive. I am me. I exist. I am Dakotah. I write. It is the quintessential act of optimism born of frustration. It is an act of courage, I think. . . . that defies oppression."

LaDonna Harris (b. 1931), is a Comanche social activist and founder of the Americans for Indian Opportunity, who helped Taos Pueblo to regain control of Blue Lake. A member of the National Museum of the American Indian, the American Civil Liberties Union, and the National Institute for Women of Color, she married a U.S. senator in the 1960s. Her autobiography, *LaDonna Harris: A Comanche Life* (2006), recounts her interractions with President Johnson.

Janet McCloud (1934–2003), also known as Yet-Si-Blue, or Talking Woman, lived up to that name. She was born into the family of Chief Seattle and, in the 1960s, began a long struggle to recover indigenous salmon fishing rights, flouted by U.S. authorities despite the treaties in place. She managed to get Marlon Brando involved in that fish war. Having become an indigenous rights activist, Janet McCloud founded WARN (Women of All Red Nations) in 1974. During the 1970s, she traveled throughout the world to spread her message of solidarity and emancipation. The crowning achievement of her life was the Sapa Dawn Center she founded in Washington state, a retreat for elders and a sweat lodge. The American Indian Movement leaders Dennis Banks and Russell Means went to pray there before their occupation of Wounded Knee in 1973. It is also the meeting place for the Indigenous Women's Network, which has remained active since McCloud's death.

Ada E. Deer, born in 1935 on the Menominee reservation in Wisconsin, became a lawyer and the first woman director of the Bureau of Indian Affairs (1993–97). She succeeded in transforming the bad relationship that had existed between that administration and Native Americans and won recognition of the rights of the Menominee as well as those of many indigenous communities in Alaska.

Wilma Mankiller (1945–2010), born in Tahlequah, Oklahoma, was the first woman elected chief of the Cherokee Nation (1985–95). The actions she took to improve the health and education of her people, and the example she set in restoring pride in their traditions, earned her the Medal of Freedom from President Bill Clinton in 1998. She tells her life story in *Mankiller: A Chief and Her People* (1993).

Mary Crow Dog (1953–2013), or Mary Brave Bird, well known in France, is the author of two autobiographies, *Lakota Woman* (1990) and *Ohitika Woman* (1993), which tell of her life on the grim Pine Ridge Reservation in South Dakota, and of the attacks by the FBI and the Bureau of Indian Affairs. The wife of Sioux leader Leonard Crow Dog, she had her moment of glory when she gave birth while under siege by federal troops at Wounded Knee, where in 1973 the American Indian Movement was commemorating the massacre that had taken place there. A made-for-TV movie, *Lakota Woman, Siege at Wounded Knee,* told her story in 1994.

Caleen Sisk (b. 1952) was elected spiritual and political chief of the Winnemem Wintu of California in 2000. The battle she has waged can be followed on the Internet. She agitated for the restoration of the salmon habitat in the McCloud River and to protect indigenous sacred sites such as the Mount Shasta volcano.

Charmaine White Face, or Zumila Wobaga, waged her own struggle, also documented on the Internet. An Oglala Sioux and civil rights activist, she coordinated the fight to defend the Black Hills of South Dakota against the irresponsible abandonment of the uranium mines and to win recognition of the rights of her people exposed to radiation.

Winona LaDuke (b. 1959) is an Anishinaabe eco-activist, economist, and writer who spearheaded the White Earth Land Recovery Project in a fight to recover territories in Minnesota. She was the Green Party's vice presidential candidate in the national elections of 1996 and 2000 and is still a prominent figure in the indigenous resistance movement.

Appendix 2
The Literary Renaissance

Mourning Dove, or Hum-isha-ma, or Christal Quintasket (1884–1936), was born in a canoe in Idaho to an Okanagan mother and an Irish father. She became the first published Indian woman writer. Her novel *Cogewea the Half-Blood: A Depiction of the Great Montana Cattle Range* (1927) tells of a mixed-blood girl on a ranch on the Flathead reservation in Montana. Mourning Dove is also the author of *Coyote Stories* (1933), a collection inspired by indigenous folklore.

Paula Gunn Allen (1939–2008), in her first novel, *The Woman Who Owned the Shadows* (1983), tells the story of a mixed-race lesbian who clashes with the world around her and reestablishes the thread of her destiny, connected to the divine spider of her ancestors. Born in Cubero, New Mexico, Allen published collections of poems, including *Life Is a Fatal Disease* (1997). She also pub-

lished the biography *Pocahontas: Medicine Woman, Spy, Entrepreneur, Diplomat* (2003) and anthologies of Indian tales, including *Spider Woman's Granddaughters: Traditional Tales and Contemporary Writing by Native American Women* (1989), which was translated into French in 1996. Her essays in feminist anthropology, *Grandmothers of the Light: A Medicine Woman's Sourcebook* (1991) and *The Sacred Hoop: Recovering the Feminine in American Indian Traditions* (1986), caused a stir in the United States. In them she writes that everything we believe we know about Native Americans was manipulated by the sexism of the first European settlers, who deliberately ignored the central role played by women in the societies they discovered. Her gynocratic theories caused controversy, but her essays remain classics on university syllabi in both Native American Studies and Women's Studies.

Janet Campbell Hale was born in 1946 to a Coeur d'Alene father and a Cree and Irish mother. She explores the cursed genealogy of American Indian women and the abuses they continue to suffer in her biography, *Bloodlines: Odyssey of a Native Daughter* (1993), and in her novels *The Owl's Song* (1974), *The Jailing of Cecelia Capture* (1985), and *Women on the Run* (1999).

Linda K. Hogan, born in Denver in 1947, is a Chickasaw poet, playwright, short story writer, and novelist. She writes historical and political essays inflected with lyricism that combine feminist and environmentalist themes with the imagery of the indigenous people and their ancestors. Her works include *The Book of Medicines* (1993), *The Sweet Breathing of Plants: Women and the Green World* (2001), and *The Woman Who Watches Over the World: A Native Memoir* (2001).

Leslie Marmon Silko, born in 1948, is known for her novel *Ceremony* (1977), which was translated into French in 1992. It tells the story of an Indian veteran of the Asia-Pacific War who becomes an alcoholic. By means of his ceremonial tradition, he finds the resources he needs to face life. "I am of mixed-breed ancestry, but what I know is Laguna," says Silko, who has also published poems (*Laguna Women*, 1974), essays (*Yellow Woman and a Beauty of the Spirit: Essays on Native American Life Today*, 1996), and a memoir (*The Turquoise Ledge*, 2010). In a book still banned in Arizona schools, she urges us to "rethink Columbus."

Beverly Hungry Wolf (Sikski-Aki, or "Black-Faced Woman") was born on the Blood Indian Reserve in Canada in 1950. She is an educator who has devoted her life to reviving the values of Blackfoot culture in her books, which include *Daughters of the Buffalo Women: Maintaining the Tribal Faith* (1997), *Children of the Sun: Stories by and about Indian Kids* (1987), and *The Ways of My Grandmothers* (1982).

Lee Maracle, born in Vancouver in 1950, was the first published Canadian Aboriginal author (*Bobbi Lee: Indian Rebel*, 1975). The author of *I Am Woman: A Native Perspective on Sociology and Feminism* (1988), an active playwright, and the former director of the Centre for Indigenous Theater in Toronto, Maracle founded a school of literature in British Columbia. She has given hundreds of lectures, conducts workshops, and serves as a consultant on self-government to the government of the First Nations of Canada.

Jamie Sams, born in 1951 of Cherokee and Seneca backgrounds, combines the oral tradition transmitted by two grandmothers and the personal healing she experiences among women elders. Her book, *The 13 Original Clan Mothers* (1993) dispenses lessons linked to the lunar cycle. Other works include *Earth Medicine: Ancestors' Ways of Harmony for Many Moons* (1994) and *Other Council Fires Were Here Before Ours* (with Twylah Hurd Nitsch, 1991), both of which have been translated into French.

Joy Harjo, born in 1951, is a Creek poet and an important voice of the Native American Renaissance. She plays the saxophone with the group Poetic Justice, writes screenplays, and directs literary reviews. American Indian women, though previously stifled by U.S. society, cannot be silenced in the end. Their voices are now carrying farther than ever.

Ofelia Zepeda, born in 1952, is the author of a collection of poems, *Ocean Power: Poems from the Desert* (1995). She holds a Ph.D. in linguistics, with a specialization in the morphology of the Tohono O'odham language. She teaches her native language at the University of Arizona and is the director of the American Indian Language Development Institute (AILDI). Zepeda also founded Sun Tracks, a press dedicated to Native American authors.

Luci Tapahonso, born in 1953, is a Navajo poet who writes in her native Diné, which she then translates into English. She celebrates women as a source of power and harmony. Her poetry collections *Saanii Dahataat: The Women Are Singing* (1993) and *Blue Horses Rush In* (1997) breathe new life into English-language poetry through their rhythms and syntax.

Louise Erdrich was born in Little Falls, Minnesota, in 1954 to an Ojibwe mother and a German father, who worked at the Bureau of Indian Affairs in North Dakota. She made a name for herself as part of the Native American literary renaissance with her first novel, *Love Medicine* (1984), written in a style that combines American hyperrealism and magical thought. *The Antelope Wife* (1998), *The Painted Drum* (2005), *The Plague of Doves* (2008), *The Red Convertible* (2009), and *Shadow Tag* (2010) are among the dozen books she has written. They depict a forgotten America living amid the ruins of Indian cultures, still under attack today. Her latest novel, *The Round House* (2012), won the National Book Award. Set on a North Dakota reservation, it tells the story of a family's disintegration following a rape, as seen through the eyes of Joey, the thirteen-year-old son, and of the long quest for justice that follows. Now the owner of a bookstore, Birchbark Books in Minnesota, Erdrich gives voice to Native American women.

Loree Boyd, of mixed Cree and Blackfoot ancestry, is the author of *Spirit Moves: The Story of Six Generations of Native Women* (1996), in which she recounts the struggles and spiritual resistance of the women in her family, from the nineteenth century to the present.

Susan Power, born in 1961, is a Sioux novelist from Chicago. Her novel *The Grass Dancer* (1994), which won the PEN/ Hemingway Award in 1996, unfolds over several generations.

Bibliography

CHAPTER 1
GUARDIANS OF TRADITION

Bunzel, Ruth L. *The Pueblo Potter: A Study of Creative Imagination in Primitive Art*. New York: Dover, 1972.

Chateaubriand, François-René de. *Oeuvres de Chateaubriand*. Vol. 3, *Les Martyrs-Voyage en Amérique*. Paris: Hachette Livres/BnF, 2013.

Deloria, Ella. *Waterlily*. Lincoln: University of Nebraska Press, 1988.

Gage, Matilda Joslyn. *Woman, Church, and State*. Amherst, N.Y.: Prometheus, 2011.

Hungry Wolf, Beverly. *The Ways of My Grandmothers*. New York: Quill, 1982.

Kehoe, Alice Beck. *America before the European Invasions*. London: Longman, 2002.

Lévi-Strauss, Claude. *L'Origine des manières de table*. Paris: Plon, 1968.

———. *The Origins of Table Manners*. Translated from the French by John and Doreen Weightman. New York: Harper & Row, 1978.

Linderman, Frank Bird. *Pretty-Shield: Medicine Woman of the Crows*. Lincoln: University of Nebraska Press, 1972.

Lurie, Nancy Oestreich, ed. *Mountain Wolf Woman, Sister of Crashing Thunder: The Autobiography of a Winnebago Indian*. Ann Arbor: University of Michigan Press, 1961.

———. *Women and the Invention of American Anthropology*. Long Grove, Ill.: Waveland, 1999.

Peterson, Susan. *The Living Tradition of María Martínez*. New York: Kodansha America, 1978.

Qoyawayma, Polingaysi. *No Turning Back: A Hopi Indian Woman's Struggle to Live in Two Worlds*. Albuquerque: University of New Mexico Press, 1977.

CHAPTER 2
AMERINDIAN SPIRITUALITY

Bettelyoun, Susan Bordeaux, and Josephine Waggoner. *With My Own Eyes: A Lakota Woman Tells Her People's History*. Lincoln: University of Nebraska Press, 1998.

Chateaubriand, François-René de. *Atala, or The Amours of Two Indians*. London: Printed for J. Lee, 1802.

Deloria, Ella. *Speaking of Indians*. Lincoln: University of Nebraska Press, 1988.

———. *Waterlily*, with an afterword by Raymond J. DeMallie. Lincoln: University of Nebraska Press, 1988.

Eastman, Charles. *Light on the Indian World: The Essential Writings of Charles Eastman (Ohiyeu)*. Bloomington, Ind.: World Wisdom, 2002.

———. *Living in Two Worlds: The American Indian Experience*. Bloomington, Ind.: World Wisdom Books, 2009.

Ferris, Jeri. *Native American Doctor: The Story of Susan LaFlesche Picotte*. Minneapolis: Carolrhoda Books, 1991.

Fitzgerald, Judith, and Michael Oren Fitzgerald. *The Spirit of Indian Women*. Bloomington, Ind.: World Wisdom Books, 2005.

Hungry Wolf, Beverly. *The Ways of My Grandmothers*. New York: Quill, 1982.

Lévi-Strauss, Claude. *Histoire de lynx*. Paris: Plon, 1991.

———. *La Pensée sauvage*. Paris: Plon, 1993.

———. *The Savage Mind*. Chicago: University of Chicago Press, 1966.

———. *The Story of Lynx*. Translated by Catherine Tihanyi. Chicago: University of Chicago Press, 1995.

Mourning Dove. *Cogewea the Half Blood: A Depiction of the Great Montana Cattle Range*. Lincoln: University of Nebraska Press, 1981.

———. *Coyote Stories*. Lincoln: University of Nebraska Press, 1990.

Radin, Paul. *The Trickster: A Study in American Indian Mythology*. New York: Schocken Books, 1987.

Standing Bear, Luther. *Land of the Spotted Eagle*. Lincoln: University of Nebraska Press, 2006.

———. *My Indian Boyhood*. Lincoln: University of Nebraska Press, 1988.

Thompson, Lucy. *To the American Indian: Reminiscences of a Yurok Woman*. Berkeley, Calif.: Heyday, 1991.

Wilson, Gilbert L. *Waheenee: An Indian Girl's Story*. Lincoln: University of Nebraska Press, 1982.

CHAPTER 3
FIRST ENCOUNTERS WITH THE SPANISH

Bucher, Bernadette. *Icon and Conquest: A Structural Analysis of the Illustrations of Bry's* Great Voyages. Chicago: University of Chicago Press, 1981.
———. *La sauvage aux seins pendants.* Paris: Hermann, 1977.
Fuentes, Carlos. *The Buried Mirror: Reflections on Spain and the New World.* Boston: Houghton Mifflin, 1992.
Le Clézi, J.M.G. *Relatión de las ceremonias y ritos y poblacíon y gobierno de los indios de la Provincia de Michoacán.* Paris: Gallimard, 1984.
Lévi-Strauss, Claude. *Nous sommes tous des cannibales.* Paris: Le Seuil, 2013.
———. *We Are All Cannibals.* New York: Columbia University Press, forthcoming.
Todorov, Tzvetan. *La conquête de l'Amérique: La question de l'autre.* Paris: Le Seuil, 1991.
———. *The Conquest of America: The Question of the Other.* New York: Harper & Row, 1984.

CHAPTER 4
FIRST ENCOUNTERS WITH THE ENGLISH

Bastide, Roger. *African Civilizations in the New World.* New York: Harper & Row, 1971.
———. *Les Amériques noires: les civilisations africaines dans le nouveu monde.* Paris: L'Harmattan, 2000.
———. *Le Prochain et le lointain.* Paris: L'Harmattan, 2003.
Gruzinski, Serge. *The Mestizo Mind: The Intellectual Dynamics of Colonization and Globalization.* New York: Routledge, 2002.
———. *La Pensée métisse.* Paris: Fayard, 1999.
Lodi, Edward. *Women in King Philip's War.* Middleboro, Mass.: Rock Village, 2012.
Plane, Ann Marie. *Colonial Intimacies: Indian Marriage in Early New England.* Ithaca, N.Y.: Cornell University Press, 2002.

CHAPTER 5
FIRST ENCOUNTERS WITH THE FRENCH

Fraïssé, Marie-Hélène. *Radisson: Indien blanc, agent double.* Paris: Actes Sud, 2008.
Havard, Gilles, and Cécile Vidal. *Histoire de l'Amérique française.* Paris: Flammarion, 2008.
Jacquin, Philippe. *Les Indiens blancs.* Paris: Payot, 1987.
Pénicault, André. *Fleur de Lys and Calumet: Being the Pénicaut Narrative of French Adventure in Louisiana.* Tuscaloosa: University of Alabama Press, 1988.
Turgeon, Laurier. *Patrimoines métissés: Contextes coloniaux et postcoloniaux.* Quebec City: Les Presses de l'Université Laval, 2003.

CHAPTER 6
A YOUNG NATION IN THE NINETEENTH CENTURY

Beaulieu, Alain, and Stéphanie Chaffray. *Représentation, métissage et pouvoir: La dynamique coloniale des échanges entre Autochtones, Européens et Canadiens (XVIe–XXe siècle).* Quebec: Presse de l'Université Laval, 2012.
Caron, Nathalie, and Naomi Wulf. *The Lewis and Clark Expedition.* Nantes: Éditions du Temps, 2005.
Hall, Edward T. *West of the Thirties: Discoveries among the Navajo and Hopi.* New York: Doubleday, 1994.
Jackson, Helen Hunt. *Ramona.* Boston: Roberts Bros., 1884.
Jemison, Mary. *The Diary of Mary Jemison, Captured by the Indians.* New York: Benchmark Books, 2001.
Kelly, Fanny. *My Captivity among the Sioux Indians.* New York: Corinth Books, 1962.
Lancaster, Richard. *Piegan: A Look from Within at the Life, Times, and Legacy of an American Indian Tribe.* Garden City, N.Y.: Doubleday, 1966.
Lewis, M., and W. Clark. *The Journals of the Lewis and Clark Expedition.* University of Nebraska Press, 2003–2007, http://lewisandclarkjournals.unl.edu/read/?_xmlsrc=lc.overview.xml&_xslsrc=LCstyles.xsl.
Namais, June. *White Captives: Gender and Ethnicity on the American Frontier.* Chapel Hill: University of North Carolina Press, 1993.
Rowlandson, Mary. *The Soveraignty and Goodness of God.* 1682.
Schoolcraft, Jane Johnston. *The Sound the Stars Make Rushing through the Sky.* Philadelphia: University of Pennsylvania Press, 2007.
Severin, Tim. *Explorers of the Mississippi.* Minneapolis: University of Minnesota Press, 2002.
Tocqueville, Alexis de. *De la démocratie en Amérique.* Paris: Folio Gallimard, 1986.
———. *Democracy in America.* 2 vols. New York: Bantam, 2000.
Wakefield, Sarah F. *Six Weeks in the Sioux Tepees: A Narrative of Indian Captivity.* Norman: University of Oklahoma Press, 1997.
Winnemucca, Sarah. *Life among the Piutes: Their Wrongs and Claims.* Boston: Cupples, Upham & Co.; New York: G. P. Putnam's Sons, 1883.

CHAPTER 7
THE EDUCATION OF AMERINDIAN CHILDREN

Adams, David Wallace. *Education for Extinction: American Indians and the Boarding School Experience 1875–1928.* Lawrence: University Press of Kansas, 1995.
Ellis, Clyde. *Boarding School Blues.* Edited by Clifford E. Trafzer, Jean A. Keller, and Lorene Sisquoc. Lincoln: University of Nebraska Press, 2006.

Gaul, Theresa Strouth. *Cherokee Sister: The Collected Writings of Catharine Brown, 1818–1823*. Lincoln: University of Nebraska, 2014.

Markstrom, Carol A. *Empowerment of North American Indian Girls: Ritual Expressions at Puberty*. Lincoln: University of Nebraska Press, 2008.

Sakiestewa Gilbert, Matthew. *Education Beyond the Mesas: Hopi Students at Sherman Institute, 1902–1929*. Lincoln: University of Nebraska Press, 2010.

Shaw, Anna Moore. *Pima Indian Legends*. Tucson: University of Arizona Press, 1968.

———. *A Pima Past*. Tucson: University of Arizona Press, 1974.

Trennert, Robert A. *The Phoenix Indian School: Forced Assimilation in Arizona, 1891–1935*. Norman: University of Oklahoma Press, 1988.

Zitkala-Ša. *American Indian Stories*. Mineola, N.Y.: Dover Publications, 2009.

———. *Dreams and Thunder: Stories, Poems, and the Sun Dance Opera*. Lincoln: University of Nebraska Press, 2001.

———. *The School Days of an Indian Girl and An Indian Teacher among Indians*. Cornwall, UK: Dodo Press, 2009.

CHAPTER 8
ORIGINS OF MODERN MASS ENTERTAINMENT

Blanchard, Pascal, Nicolas Bancel, Sandrine Lemaire, Gilles Boëtsh, and Eric Deroo. *Zoos humains et exhibitions coloniales*. Paris: La Découverte, 2011.

Trachtenberg, Alan. *Shades of Hiawatha: Staging Indians, Making Americans, 1880–1930*. New York: Hill and Wang, 2005.

CHAPTER 9
AMERICAN INDIAN WOMEN IN HOLLYWOOD

Bazin, André. *Qu'est-ce que le cinéma?* 4 vols. Paris: Cerf, 1958–62.

———. *What Is Cinema?* 2 vols. Translation of selections from the French text by Hugh Gray. Berkeley: University of California Press, 1967–71.

Bellour, Raymond. *Le Western*. Paris: Gallimard, 1993.

Marubbio, Elise. *Killing the Indian Maiden: Images of Native American Women in Film*. Lexington: University Press of Kentucky, 2006.

Rieupeyrout, Jean-Louis. *Le Western ou le cinéma américain par excellence*. Cerf, 1953.

Tavernier, Bertrand. *Amis américains: Entretiens avec les grands auteurs d'Hollywood*. Arles: Actes Sud, 2008.

EPILOGUE
THE RESISTANCE OF AMERICAN INDIAN WOMEN AND APPENDICES

Allen, Paula Gunn. *Grandmothers of the Light: A Medicine Woman's Sourcebook*. Boston: Beacon Press, 1991.

———. *Life Is a Fatal Disease: Selected Poems 1962–1995*. Albuquerque, N.M.: West End Press, 1997.

———. *Pocahontas: Medicine Woman, Spy, Entrepreneur, Diplomat*. San Francisco: Harper San Francisco, 2003.

———. *The Sacred Hoop: Recovering the Feminine in American Indian Traditions*. Boston: Beacon Press, 1992.

———, ed. *Spider Woman's Granddaughters: Traditional Tales and Contemporary Writing by Native American Women*. Boston: Beacon Press, 1989.

———. *The Woman Who Owned the Shadows*. San Francisco: Spinsters, Ink, 1983.

Boyd, Loree. *Spirit Moves: The Story of Six Generations of Native Women*. Novato, Calif.: New World Library, 1996.

Brave Bird, Mary. *Lakota Woman*. New York: Grove Weidenfeld, 1990.

———. *Ohitika Woman*. New York: Grove Press, 1993.

Broker, Ignatia. *Night Flying Woman: An Ojibway Narrative*. St. Paul: Minnesota Historical Society Press, 1983.

Clastres, Pierre. *Recherches d'anthropologie politique*. Paris: Le Seuil, 1980.

Cook-Lynn, Elizabeth. *Anti-Indianism in Modern America: A Voice from Tatekeya's Earth*. Urbana: University of Illinois Press, 2001.

———. *A Separate Country: Postcoloniality and American Indian Nations*. Lubbock: Texas Tech University Press, 2012.

Cook-Lynn, Elizabeth, and Mario Gonzalez. *The Politics of Hallowed Ground: Wounded Knee and the Struggle for Indian Sovereignty*. Urbana: University of Illinois Press, 1999.

Erdrich, Louise. *The Antelope Wife*. New York: HarperFlamingo, 1998.

———. *Love Medicine*. New York: Holt, Rinehart, and Winston, 1984.

———. *The Painted Drum*. New York: HarperCollins, 2005.

———. *The Plague of Doves*. New York: HarperCollins, 2008.

———. *The Red Convertible*. New York: HarperCollins, 2009.

———. *The Round House*. New York: Harper, 2012.

———. *Shadow Tag*. New York: Harper, 2010.

Hale, Janet Campbell. *Bloodlines: Odyssey of a Native Daughter*. Tucson: University of Arizona Press, 1998.

———. *The Jailing of Cecelia Capture*. Albuquerque: University of New Mexico Press, 1987.

———. *The Owl's Song*. New York: HarperPerennial, 1995.

———. *Women on the Run*. Moscow: University of Idaho Press, 1999.

Harris, LaDonna. *A Comanche Life*. Lincoln, Nebr.: Bison Books, 2006.

Hogan, Linda K. *The Book of Medicines*. Minneapolis: Coffee House Press, 1993.

———. *Indios: A Poem to be Spoken*. San Antonio, Tex.: Wings Press, 2011.

———, ed. *The Inner Journey: Views from Native Traditions*. Sandpoint, Id.: Morning Light Press, 2009.

———. *People of the Whale*. New York: W.W. Norton, 2008.

———. *Rounding the Human Corners*. Minneapolis: Coffee House Press, 2008.

———. *Walk Gently upon the Earth*. Lulu.com, 2010.

———. *The Woman Who Watches Over the World: A Native Memoir*. New York: W.W. Norton, 2001.

Hogan, Linda K., and Brenda Peterson, eds. *The Sweet Breathing of Plants: Women and the Green World*. New York: North Point Press 2001.

Hungry Wolf, Beverly. *Blackfoot Craftworker's Book*. Summertown, Tenn.: Book Publishing Company, 1993.

———. *Children of the Sun: Stories by and about Indian Kids*. New York: William Morrow, 1987.

———. *Daughters of the Buffalo Women: Maintaining the Tribal Faith*. Summertown, Tenn.: Book Publishing Company, 1997.

———. *Indian Tribes of the Northern Rockies*. Summertown, Tenn.: Book Publishing Company, 1991.

———. *Shadows of the Buffalo: A Family Odyssey among the Indians*. New York: William Morrow, 1983.

———. *Siksika: A Blackfoot Legacy*. Invermere, B.C.: Good Medicine Books, 1979.

Jaulin, Robert. *La paix blanche*. Paris: Le Seuil, 1970.

Mankiller, Wilma. *Mankiller: A Chief and Her People*. New York: St. Martin's, 2001.

Maracle, Lee. *Bobbi Lee: Indian Rebel*. Toronto: Woman's Press of Canada, 1990.

———. *I Am Woman: A Native Perspective on Sociology and Feminism*. Vancouver: Press Gang Publishers, 1988.

Medicine, Beatrice. *Learning to Be an Anthropologist and Remaining "Native": Selected Writings*. Urbana: University of Illinois Press, 2001.

———. *The Native American Woman: A Perspective*. Austin, Tex.: National Educational Laboratory Publishers, 1978.

Medicine, Beatrice, and Patricia Albers. *The Hidden Half: Studies of Plains Indian Women*. Washington, D.C.: University Press of America, 1983.

Power, Susan. *The Grass Dancer*. New York: Putnam's, 1994.

Sams, Jamie. *Earth Medicine: Ancestors' Ways of Harmony for Many Moons*. San Francisco: HarperSanFrancisco, 1994.

———. *The 13 Original Clan Mothers: Your Sacred Path to Discovering the Gifts, Talents, and Abilities of the Feminine through the Ancient Teachings of the Sisterhood*. San Francisco: HarperSanFrancisco, 1993.

Sams, Jamie, and Twylah Hurd Nitsch. *Other Council Fires Were Here Before Ours*. San Francisco: HarperSanFrancisco, 1991.

Silko, Leslie Marmon. *Ceremony*. New York: Viking Press, 1977.

———. *Laguna Woman*. Greenfield Center, N.Y.: Greenfield Review Press, 1974.

———. *The Turquoise Ledge: A Memoir*. New York: Viking, 2010.

———. *Yellow Woman and a Beauty of the Spirit: Essays on Native American Life Today*. New York: Simon and Schuster, 1996.

Stewart, Irene. *A Voice in Her Tribe: A Navajo Woman's Own Story*. Socorro, N.M.: Ballena Press, 1981.

Swann, Brian, and Arnold Krupat, eds. *I Tell You Now: Autobiographical Essays by Native American Writers*. Lincoln, Nebr.: Bison Books, 1989.

Tapahonso, Luci. *Blue Horses Rush In: Poems and Stories*. Tucson: University of Arizona Press, 1997.

———. *Saanii Dahataat: The Women Are Singing*. Tucson: University of Arizona Press, 1993.

Zepeda, Ofelia. *Ocean Power: Poems from the Desert*. Tucson: University of Arizona Press, 1995.

Index

Page numbers in *italics* refer to illustrations.

Image Credits